Chain Gang—
The Chemistry of Polymers

Science in Our World
Volume Five

Developed in collaboration with

Quantum Chemical Corporation

Series Editor
Mickey Sarquis, Director
Center for Chemical Education

©1995 by Terrific Science Press
ISBN 1-883822-13-0 First printed 1995 Revised and reprinted 1997
All rights reserved. Printed in the United States of America.

This project was supported, in part, by the National Science Foundation. Any opinions, findings, and conclusions or recommendations expressed in this material are those of the authors and do not necessarily reflect the views of the National Science Foundation. The Government has certain rights to this material. This material is based upon work supported by the National Science Foundation under Grant No. TPE-9153930.

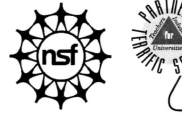

Center for
Chemical Education

D1088586

This monograph is intended for use by teachers, chemists, and properly supervised students. Teachers and other users must develop and follow procedures for the safe handling, use, and disposal of chemicals in accordance with local and state regulations and requirements. The cautions, warnings, and safety reminders associated with the doing of experiments and activities involving the use of chemicals and equipment contained in this publication have been compiled from sources believed to be reliable and to represent the best opinion on the subject as of 1995. However, no warranty, guarantee, or representation is made by the editor, contributors, Quantum Chemical Corporation, or the Terrific Science Press as to the correctness or sufficiency of any information herein. Neither the editor, contributors, Quantum Chemical Corporation, or Terrific Science Press assumes any responsibility or liability for the use of the information herein, nor can it be assumed that all necessary warnings and precautionary measures are contained in this publication. Other or additional information or measures may be required or desirable because of particular or exceptional conditions or circumstances, or because of new or changed legislation.

Contributors

Industrial Mentors

Mark Sabo
Assistant Director, Partnership for the Advancement of Chemical Technology
Center for Chemical Education, Miami University
Middletown, Ohio
(formerly of Quantum Chemical Corporation, Cincinnati, Ohio)

Sue Matz
Research Specialist, Quantum Chemical Corporation
Cincinnati, Ohio

Academic Mentor

Neil Danielson
Chemistry Professor, Miami University
Oxford, Ohio

Peer Mentor

Sandy Van Natta
Eighth-Grade Teacher, White Oak Middle School
Cincinnati, Ohio

Principal Investigators

Mickey Sarquis   Miami University, Middletown, Ohio
Jim Coats   Dow Chemical USA (retired), Findlay, Ohio
Dan McLoughlin   Xavier University, Cincinnati, Ohio
Rex Bucheit   Fillmore Elementary School, Hamilton, Ohio

Partners for Terrific Science Advisory Board

Ruby L. Bryant   Colonel White High School, Dayton, Ohio
Rex Bucheit   Fillmore Elementary School (ex-officio), Hamilton, Ohio
Jim Coats   Dow Chemical USA (retired, ex-officio), Findlay, Ohio
Dick French   Quantum Chemical Corporation (retired, ex-officio), Cincinnati, Ohio
Judy Gilbert   BP America/Ohio Chemical Council, Lima, Ohio
Linda Jester   John XXIII Elementary School, Middletown, Ohio
James C. Letton   Procter & Gamble, Cincinnati, Ohio
Ted J. Logan   Procter & Gamble, Ross, Ohio
Ken Lohr   Hoechst Marion Roussel, Inc. (retired), Cincinnati, Ohio
Alan McClelland   Delaware Science Alliance (DuPont, retired), Rockland, Delaware
                       (deceased)
Dan McLoughlin   Xavier University (ex-officio), Cincinnati, Ohio
Raymond C. Odioso   R.C. Odioso Consultants, Inc. (Drackett, retired), Cincinnati, Ohio,
                       St. Petersburg Beach, Florida
Tom Runyan   Garfield Alternative School, Middletown, Ohio
Ken Wilkinson   Hilton Davis Company (retired), Cincinnati, Ohio
John P. Williams   Miami University Hamilton, Hamilton, Ohio
Regina Wolterman   Our Lady of Lourdes Elementary School, Cincinnati, Ohio

Table of Contents

Acknowledgments

The authors and editor wish to thank the following individuals who have contributed to the development of the *Science in Our World* series of Teacher Resource Modules.

Terrific Science Press Design and Production Team
Susan Gertz, Amy Stander, Lisa Taylor, Thomas Nackid, Stephen Gentle, Vickie Fultz, Anne Munson, Amy Hudepohl, Andrea Nolan, Pamela Mason

Reviewers

Paul Barnard	Quantum Chemical Corporation, Cincinnati, Ohio
G. Lynn Carlson	University of Wisconsin, Kenosha, Wisconsin
Susan Hershberger	Miami University, Oxford, Ohio
Baird Lloyd	Miami University, Middletown, Ohio
Mark Sabo	Miami University, Middletown, Ohio
Dave Tomlin	Wright Patterson Air Force Base, Dayton, Ohio
Linda Woodward	University of Southwestern Louisiana, Lafayette, Louisiana

Center for Chemical Education Staff

Mickey Sarquis, Director
Bruce L. Peters, Jr., Associate Director
Billie Gerzema, Administrative Assistant

Assistants to Director

Susan Gertz	Mark Sabo
Lynn Hogue	Lisa Meeder Turnbull

Project Coordinators and Managers

Richard French	Andrea Nolan
Betty Kibbey	Ginger Smith
Carl Morgan	Amy Stander

Research Associates and Assistants

Kersti Cox	Pamela Mason
Stephen Gentle	Anne Munson
Susan Hershberger	Thomas Nackid
Amy Hudepohl	Michael Parks
Robert Hunter	Lisa Taylor

Program Secretaries

Victoria Burton	Ruth Willis

Graduate Assistants

Michelle Diebolt	Richard Rischling
Nancy Grim	Michella Stultz

Foreword

Chain Gang—The Chemistry of Polymers is one of the *Science in Our World* Teacher Resource Modules. This set is aimed at enabling teachers to introduce their students to the concepts and processes of industrial chemistry and to relate these concepts to the consumer products students encounter daily. These hands-on, problem-solving activities help connect science lessons with real life.

Developed as a collaborative effort between industrial, academic, and teacher peer mentors in the *Partners for Terrific Science* program, this module provides background information on the polymer industry and Quantum Chemical Corporation's role in this industry, as well as a content review of polymer science and pedagogical strategies. The activities in this module have been tested by participants in *Partners* programs and by *Partners* teachers in their classrooms, and reviewed by experts in the field to help ensure accuracy, safety, and pedagogical effectiveness.

Partners for Terrific Science, established in 1986, is an industrial/academic partnership that facilitates interaction among classroom teachers, industrial scientists and engineers, and university chemistry faculty to make science education more interesting, relevant, and understandable for all students. The partnership is supported by the Ohio Chemical Council and its more than 100 members, the National Science Foundation, the U.S. Department of Education, the Ohio Board of Regents, the American Chemical Society—Cincinnati Section, Miami University, and over 50 private-sector partners. Quantum Chemical Corporation has generously contributed to the production of this module.

The Teacher Resource Modules have been developed especially for teachers who want to use industry-based physical science activities in the classroom, but who may not have been able to attend a *Partners* workshop at the Miami site or one of the Affiliate sites nationwide. We want to thank all the contributors, participants, and mentors who made this publication possible.

We hope you will find that these Teacher Resource Modules provide you with a useful and exciting way to involve your students in doing chemistry through integrated real-world themes. We welcome your comments at any time and are interested in learning about especially successful uses of these materials.

Mickey Sarquis, Director
Center for Chemical Education
July 1995

The Center for Chemical Education

Built on a tradition of quality programming, materials development, and networking between academia and industry, Miami University's Center for Chemical Education (CCE) encompasses a multifaceted collaboration of cross-grade-level and interdisciplinary initiatives begun in the mid-1980s as Terrific Science Programs. These initiatives are linked through the centrality of chemistry to the goal of fostering quality hands-on, minds-on science education for all students. CCE activities include credit coursework and other opportunities for educators at all levels; K–12 student programs; undergraduate, graduate, and postgraduate programs in chemical education; materials development, including teacher resource materials, program handbooks, and videos; public outreach efforts and networking to foster new and existing partnerships among classroom teachers, university-based science educators, industrial scientists, and professional societies.

Professional Development for Educators

Credit Courses
: The Center for Chemical Education offers a variety of summer and academic-year workshop-style courses for K–12 and college teachers. While each workshop has a unique focus, all reflect current pedagogical approaches in science education, cutting-edge academic and industrial research topics, and classroom applications for teachers and students. Short courses provide opportunities for educators to enrich their science teaching in a limited amount of time. All courses offer graduate credit.

Non-Credit Courses
: Academies allow CCE graduates and other teachers to attend special one-day sessions presented by leading science educators from around the United States. Offerings include seminars, mini-workshops, and share-and-swap sessions.

Internships
: Through 8- to 10-week summer internships, program graduates work as members of industrial teams to gain insight into the day-to-day workings of industrial laboratories, enabling them to bring real-world perspectives into the classroom.

Fellowships
: Master teachers at primary, secondary, and college levels do research in chemical education and undertake curriculum and materials development as Teacher Fellows with the Center for Chemical Education. Fellowships are available for the summer and the academic year.

K–12 Student Programming

Summer Camps
: A variety of summer camps are available to area elementary, middle, and high school students. These camps not only provide laboratory-based enrichment for students, but also enable educators in summer courses to apply their knowledge of hands-on exploration and leadership skills. Satellite camps are offered at affiliated sites throughout the country.

Science Carnivals
: Carnivals challenge elementary school students with hands-on science in a non-traditional atmosphere, encouraging them to apply the scientific method to activities that demonstrate scientific principles. Sponsoring teachers and their students host these carnivals for other students in their districts.

Super Saturday Science Sessions	High school students are introduced to industrial and research applications of science and technology through special Saturday sessions that involve the students in experiment-based problem-solving. Topics have included waste management, environmental sampling, engineering technology, paper science, chemical analysis, microbiology, and many others.
Ambassador Program	Professional chemists, technicians, and engineers, practicing and recently retired, play important roles as classroom ambassadors for high school and two-year college students. Ambassadors not only serve as classroom resources, but they are also available as consultants when a laboratory scenario calls for outside expertise; they mentor special projects both in and out of the classroom; and they are available for career counseling and professional advice.

Undergraduate and Graduate Student Programming

Teaching Science with TOYS Undergraduate Course	This undergraduate course replicates the Teaching Science with TOYS teacher inservice program for the preservice audience. Students participate in hands-on physics and chemistry sessions.
General Chemistry Initiative	This effort is aimed at more effectively including chemical analysis and problem solving in the two-year college curriculum. To accomplish this goal, we are developing and testing discovery-based laboratory scenarios and take-home lecture supplements that illustrate topics in chemistry through activities beyond the classroom. In addition to demonstrating general chemistry concepts, these activities also involve students in critical-thinking and group problem-solving skills used by professional chemists in industry and academia.
Chemical Technology Curriculum Development	Curriculum and materials development efforts highlight the collaboration between college and high school faculty and industrial partners. These efforts will lead to the dissemination of a series of activity-based monographs, including detailed instructions for discovery-based investigations that challenge students to apply principles of chemical technology, chemical analysis, and Good Laboratory Practices in solving problems that confront practicing chemical technicians in the workplace.
Other Undergraduate Activities	The CCE has offered short courses/seminars for undergraduates that are similar in focus and pedagogy to CCE teacher/faculty enhancement programming. In addition, CCE staff members provide Miami University students with opportunities to interact in area schools through public outreach efforts and to undertake independent study projects in chemical education.
Degree Program	Miami's Department of Chemistry offers both a Ph.D. and M.S. in Chemical Education for graduate students who are interested in becoming teachers of chemistry in situations where a comprehensive knowledge of advanced chemical concepts is required and where acceptable scholarly activity can include the pursuit of chemical education research.

Educational Materials

The Terrific Science Press publications have emerged from CCE's work with classroom teachers of grades K–12 and college in graduate-credit, workshop-style inservice courses. Before being released, our materials undergo extensive classroom testing by teachers working with students at the targeted grade level, peer review by experts in the field for accuracy and safety, and editing by a staff of technical writers for clear, accurate, and consistent materials lists and procedures. The following is a list of Terrific Science Press publications to date.

Science Activities for Elementary Classrooms (1986)

Science SHARE is a resource for busy K–6 teachers to enable them to use hands-on science activities in their classrooms. The activities included use common, everyday materials and complement or supplement any existing science curriculum. This book was published in collaboration with Flinn Scientific, Inc.

Polymers All Around You! (1992)

This monograph focuses on the uses of polymer chemistry in the classroom. It includes several multi-part activities dealing with topics such as polymer recycling and polymers and polarized light. This monograph was published in collaboration with POLYED, a joint education committee of two divisions of the American Chemical Society: the Division of Polymer Chemistry and the Division of the Polymeric Materials: Science and Engineering.

Fun with Chemistry Volume 2 (1993)

The second volume of a set of two hands-on activity collections, this book contains classroom-tested science activities that enhance teaching, are fun to do, and help make science relevant to young students. This book was published in collaboration with the Institute for Chemical Education (ICE), University of Wisconsin-Madison.

Santa's Scientific Christmas (1993)

In this school play for elementary students, Santa's elves teach him the science behind his toys. The book and accompanying video provide step-by-step instructions for presenting the play. The book also contains eight fun, hands-on science activities to do in the classroom.

Teaching Chemistry with TOYS Teaching Physics with TOYS (1995)

Each volume contains more than 40 activities for grades K–9. Both were developed in collaboration with and tested by classroom teachers from around the country. These volumes were published in collaboration with McGraw-Hill, Inc.

Palette of Color Monograph Series (1995)

The three monographs in this series present the chemistry behind dye colors and show how this chemistry is applied in "real-world" settings:
- The Chemistry of Vat Dyes
- The Chemistry of Natural Dyes
- The Chemistry of Food Dyes

Science in Our World Teacher Resource Modules (1995)

Each volume of this five-volume set presents chemistry activities based on a specific industry—everything from pharmaceuticals to polymers. Developed as a result of the *Partners for Terrific Science* program, this set explores the following topics and industries:
- Science Fare—Chemistry at the Table (Procter & Gamble)
- Strong Medicine—Chemistry at the Pharmacy (Hoechst Marion Roussel, Inc.)
- Dirt Alert—The Chemistry of Cleaning (Diversey Corporation)
- Fat Chance—The Chemistry of Lipids (Henkel Corporation, Emery Group)
- Chain Gang—The Chemistry of Polymers (Quantum Chemical Corporation)

Teaching Physical Science through Children's Literature (1996)	This book offers 20 complete lessons for teaching hands-on, discovery-oriented physical science in the elementary classroom using children's fiction and nonfiction books as an integral part of that instruction. Each lesson in this book is a tightly integrated learning episode with a clearly defined science content objective supported and enriched by all facets of the lesson, including reading of both fiction and nonfiction, writing, and, where appropriate, mathematics. Along with the science content objectives, many process objectives are woven into every lesson.
Teaching Science with TOYS Teacher Resource Modules (1996, 1997)	The modules in this series are designed as instructional units focusing on a given theme or content area in chemistry or physics. Built around a collection of grade-level-appropriate TOYS activities, each Teacher Resource Module also includes a content review and pedagogical strategies section. Volumes listed below were published or are forthcoming in collaboration with McGraw-Hill, Inc.

- Exploring Matter with TOYS: Using and Understanding the Senses
- Investigating Solids, Liquids, and Gases with TOYS: States of Matter and Changes of State
- Transforming Energy with TOYS: Mechanical Energy and Energy Conversions

Terrific Science Network

Affiliates	College and district affiliates to CCE programs disseminate ideas and programming throughout the United States. Program affiliates offer support for local teachers, including workshops, resource/symposium sessions, and inservices; science camps; and college courses.
Industrial Partners	We collaborate directly with over 40 industrial partners, all of whom are fully dedicated to enhancing the quality of science education for teachers and students in their communities and beyond. A list of corporations and organizations that support *Partners for Terrific Science* is included on the following page.
Outreach	On the average, graduates of CCE professional development programs report reaching about 40 other teachers through district inservices and other outreach efforts they undertake. Additionally, graduates, especially those in facilitator programs, institute their own local student programs. CCE staff also undertake significant outreach through collaboration with local schools, service organizations, professional societies, and museums.
Newsletters	CCE newsletters provide a vehicle for network communication between program graduates, members of industry, and other individuals active in chemical and science education. Newsletters contain program information, hands-on science activities, teacher resources, and ideas on how to integrate hands-on science into the curriculum.

For more information about any of the CCE initiatives, contact us at

Center for Chemical Education
4200 East University Blvd.
Middletown, OH 45042
513/727-3318
FAX: 513/727-3223
e-mail: *CCE@muohio.edu*
http://www.muohio.edu/~ccecwis/

Partnership Network

We appreciate the dedication and contributions of the following corporations and organizations, who together make *Partners for Terrific Science* a true partnership for the betterment of chemical education for all teachers and students.

Partners in the Private Sector

A & B Foundry, Inc.
Aeronca, Inc.
Ag Renu
Air Products and Chemicals, Inc.
Armco, Inc.
Armco Research and Technology
ARW Polywood
Ashland Chemical Company
Bank One
BASF
Bay West Paper Corporation
Black Clawson Company
BP America: BP Oil, BP Chemicals
Coats & Clark
Crystal Tissue Company
DataChem Laboratories, Inc.
Diversey Corporation
Ronald T. Dodge Company
Dover Chemical Corporation
EG&G Mound Applied Technologies
Fluor Daniel Fernald, Inc.
Formica
Golden Pond Resources

Henkel Corporation, Emery Group
Hewlett-Packard Company
Hilton Davis Company
Hoechst Marion Roussel, Inc.
Inland Container Corporation
Jefferson Smurfit Corporation
JLJ, Inc.
Magnode Corporation
Middletown Paperboard Corporation
Middletown Regional Hospital
Middletown Wastewater Treatment Plant
Middletown Water Treatment Plant
Miller Brewing Company
The Monsanto Fund
Owens Corning Science & Technology Laboratories
The Procter & Gamble Company
Quality Chemicals
Quantum Chemical Corporation
Rumpke Waste Removal/Recycling
Shepherd Chemical Company
Shepherd Color Company
Square D Company
Sun Chemical Corporation

Partners in the Public Sector

Hamilton County Board of Education
Indiana Tech-Prep
Miami University
Middletown Clean Community
National Institute of Environmental Health Sciences
National Science Foundation
Ohio Board of Regents

Ohio Department of Education
Ohio Environmental Protection Agency
Ohio Tech-Prep
State Board for Technical and Comprehensive Education, Columbia, SC
US Department of Education
US Department of Energy, Cincinnati, OH

Professional Societies

American Association of Physics Teachers
African American Math-Science Coalition
American Chemical Society— Central Regional Council
American Chemical Society— Cincinnati Section
American Chemical Society— Dayton Section
American Chemical Society—POLYED
American Chemical Society— Technician Division
American Chemical Society, Washington, DC

American Institute of Chemical Engineers
Chemical Manufacturers Association
Chemistry Teachers Club of New York
Intersocietal Polymer and Plastics Education Initiative
Minorities in Mathematics, Science and Engineering
National Organization of Black Chemists and Chemical Engineers—Cincinnati Section
National Science Teachers Association
Ohio Chemical Council
Science Education Council of Ohio
Society of Plastics Engineers

More than 3,000 teachers are involved in and actively benefiting from this Network.

An Invitation to Industrial Chemists

It is not unusual to hear children say they want to be doctors, astronauts, or teachers when they grow up. It is easy for children to see adults they admire doing these jobs in books, on television, and in real life. But where are our aspiring chemists? The chemist portrayed on television often bears close resemblance to Mr. Hyde: an unrealistic and unfortunate role model.

Children delight in learning and enjoy using words like "stegosaurus" and "pterodactyl." Wouldn't it be wonderful to hear words like "chromatography" and "density" used with the same excitement? You could be introducing elementary school students to these words for the first time. And imagine a 10-year-old child coming home from school and announcing, "When I grow up, I want to be a chemist!" You can be the one responsible for such enthusiasm. By taking the time to visit and interact with an elementary or middle school classroom as a guest scientist, you can become the chemist who makes the difference.

You are probably aware that many non-chemists, including many prehigh school teachers, find science in general (and chemistry in particular) mysterious and threatening. When given a chance, both teachers and students can enjoy transforming the classroom into a laboratory and exploring like real scientists. Consider being the catalyst for this transformation.

Unlike magicians, scientists attempt to find explanations for why and how things happen. Challenge students to join in on the fun of searching for explanations. At the introductory level, it is far more important to provide non-threatening opportunities for the students to postulate "why?" than it is for their responses to be absolutely complete. If the accepted explanation is too complex to discuss, maybe the emphasis of the presentation is wrong. For example, discussions focusing on the fact that a color change can be an indication of a chemical reaction may be more useful than a detailed explanation of the reaction mechanisms involved.

Because science involves the process of discovery, it is equally important to let the students know that not all the answers are known and that they too can make a difference. Teachers should be made to feel that responses like "I don't know. What do you think?" or "Let's find out together," are acceptable. It is also important to point out that not everyone's results will be the same. Reinforce the idea that a student's results are not wrong just because they are different from a classmate's results.

While using the term "chemistry," try relating the topics to real-life experiences and integrating topics into non-science areas. After all, chemistry is all around us, not just in the chemistry lab.

When interacting with students, take care to involve all of them. It is very worthwhile to spend time talking informally with small groups or individual students before, during, or after your presentation. It is important to convey the message that chemistry is for all who are willing to apply themselves to the questions before them. Chemistry is neither sexist, racist, nor frightening.

For more information on becoming involved in the classroom and a practical and valuable discussion of some do's and don'ts, a resource is available. The American Chemical Society Education Division has an informative booklet and video called *Chemists in the Classroom.* You may request this package for $20.00 from: Education Division, American Chemical Society, 1155 Sixteenth Street NW, Washington, DC 20036, 800/227-5558.

How to Use This Teacher Resource Module

This section is an introduction to the Teacher Resource Module and its organization. The industry featured in this module is the polymer industry.

How Is This Resource Module Organized?

The Teacher Resource Module is organized into the following main sections: How to Use This Teacher Resource Module (this section), Background for Teachers, Using the Activities in the Classroom, and Activities and Demonstrations. Background for Teachers includes Overview of the Polymer Industry, Quantum Chemical Corporation, and Content Review. Using the Activities in the Classroom includes Pedagogical Strategies, an Annotated List of Activities and Demonstrations, and a Curriculum Placement Guide. The following paragraphs provide a brief overview of the *Chain Gang—The Chemistry of Polymers* module.

Background for Teachers

Overviews of the polymer industry and Quantum Chemical Corporation's role in the industry provide information on the industrial aspect of these activities. The Content Review section is intended to provide you, the teacher, with an introduction to (or a review of) the concepts covered in the module. The material in this section (and in the individual activity explanations) intentionally gives you information at a level beyond what you will present to your students. You can then evaluate how to adjust the content presentation for your own students.

The Content Review section in this module covers the following topics:
- Carbon Bonding
- Polymers from Monomers
- Polyethylene
- Types of Polymerization Reactions
- Some Interesting Characteristics of Polymers
- Polymer Manufacturing Techniques
- Polymer Recycling Codes

Using the Activities in the Classroom

The Pedagogical Strategies section is intended to provide ideas for effectively teaching a unit on the polymer industry. It suggests a variety of ways to incorporate the industry-based activities presented in the module into your curriculum. The Annotated List of Activities and Demonstrations and the Curriculum Placement Guide provide recommended grade levels, descriptions of the activities, and recommended placement of the activities within a typical curriculum.

Activities and Demonstrations

Each module activity provides complete instructions for conducting the activity in your classroom. These activities have been classroom-tested by teachers like yourself and have been demonstrated to be practical, safe, and effective in the typical classroom. The following information is provided for each activity:

Recommended Grade Level: The grade levels at which the activity will be most effective are listed.

Group Size:	The optimal student group size is listed.
Time for Preparation:	This includes time to set up for the activity before beginning with the students.
Time for Procedure:	An estimated time for conducting the activity is listed. This time estimate is based on feedback from classroom testing, but your time may vary depending on your classroom and teaching style.
Materials:	Materials are listed for each part of the activity, divided into amounts per class, per group, and per student.
Resources:	Sources for difficult-to-find materials are listed.
Safety and Disposal:	Special safety and/or disposal procedures are listed if required.
Getting Ready:	Information is provided in Getting Ready when preparation is needed prior to beginning the activity with the students.
Opening Strategy:	A strategy for introducing the topic to be covered and for gaining the students' interest is suggested.
Procedure:	The steps in the Procedure are directed toward you, the teacher, and include cautions and suggestions where appropriate.
Variations and Extensions:	Variations are alternative methods for doing the Procedure. Extensions are methods for furthering student understanding.
Discussion:	Possible questions for students are provided.
Explanation:	The Explanation is written to you, the teacher, and is intended to be modified for students.
Key Science Concepts:	Targeted key science topics are listed.
Cross-Curricular Integration:	Cross-Curricular Integration provides suggestions for integrating the science activity with other areas of the curriculum.
References:	References used to write this activity are listed.

Notes and safety cautions are included in activities as needed and are indicated by the following icons and type style:

Notes are preceded by an arrow.

Cautions are preceded by an exclamation point.

Employing Appropriate Safety Procedures

Experiments, demonstrations, and hands-on activities add relevance, fun, and excitement to science education at any level. However, even the simplest activity can become dangerous when the proper safety precautions are ignored or when the activity is done incorrectly or performed by students without proper supervision. While the activities in this book include cautions, warnings, and safety reminders from sources believed to be reliable, and while the text has been extensively reviewed, it is your responsibility to develop and follow procedures for the safe execution of any activity you choose to do and for the safe handling, use, and disposal of chemicals in accordance with local and state regulations and requirements.

Safety First

- Collect and read the Materials Safety Data Sheets (MSDS) for all of the chemicals used in your experiments. MSDS's provide physical property data, toxicity information, and handling and disposal specifications for chemicals. They can be obtained upon request from manufacturers and distributors of these chemicals. In fact, MSDS's are often shipped with chemicals when they are ordered. These should be collected and made available to students, faculty, or parents for information about specific chemicals in these activities.

- Read and follow the American Chemical Society Minimum Safety Guidelines for Chemical Demonstrations on the next page. Remember that you are a role model for your students—your attention to safety will help them develop good safety habits while assuring that everyone has fun with these activities.

- Read each activity carefully and observe all safety precautions and disposal procedures. Determine and follow all local and state regulations and requirements.

- Never attempt an activity if you are unfamiliar or uncomfortable with the procedures or materials involved. Consult a high school or college chemistry teacher or an industrial chemist for advice or ask him or her to perform the activity for your class. These people are often delighted to help.

- Always practice activities yourself before using them with your class. This is the only way to become thoroughly familiar with an activity, and familiarity will help prevent potentially hazardous (or merely embarrassing) mishaps. In addition, you may find variations that will make the activity more meaningful to your students.

- Undertake activities only at the recommended grade levels and only with adult supervision.

- You, your assistants, and any students participating in the preparation for or doing of the activity must wear safety goggles if indicated in the activity and at any other time you deem necessary.

- Special safety instructions are not given for everyday classroom materials being used in a typical manner. Use common sense when working with hot, sharp, or breakable objects. Keep tables or desks covered to avoid stains. Keep spills cleaned up to avoid falls.

- When an activity requires students to smell a substance, instruct them to smell the substance as follows: hold its container approximately 6 inches from the nose and, using the free hand, gently waft the air above the open container toward the nose. Never smell an unknown substance by placing it directly under the nose. (See figure.)

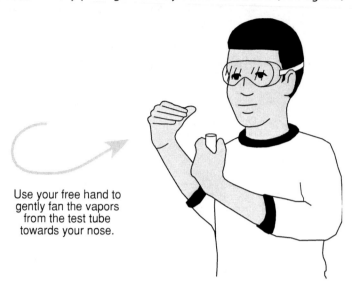

Use your free hand to gently fan the vapors from the test tube towards your nose.

Wafting procedure—Carefully wave the air above the open container towards your nose. Avoid hitting the container in the process.

- Caution students never to taste anything made in the laboratory and not to place their fingers in their mouths after handling laboratory chemicals.

ACS Minimum Safety Guidelines for Chemical Demonstrations

This section outlines safety procedures that Chemical Demonstrators must follow at all times.

1. Know the properties of the chemicals and the chemical reactions involved in all demonstrations presented.

2. Comply with all local rules and regulations.

3. Wear appropriate eye protection for all chemical demonstrations.

4. Warn the members of the audience to cover their ears whenever a loud noise is anticipated.

5. Plan the demonstration so that harmful quantities of noxious gases (e.g., NO_2, SO_2, H_2S) do not enter the local air supply.

6. Provide safety shield protection wherever there is the slightest possibility that a container, its fragments or its contents could be propelled with sufficient force to cause personal injury.

7. Arrange to have a fire extinguisher at hand whenever the slightest possibility for fire exists.

8. Do not taste or encourage spectators to taste any non-food substance.

9. Never use demonstrations in which parts of the human body are placed in danger (such as placing dry ice in the mouth or dipping hands into liquid nitrogen).

10. Do not use "open" containers of volatile, toxic substances (e.g., benzene, CCl_4, CS_2, formaldehyde) without adequate ventilation as provided by fume hoods.

11. Provide written procedure, hazard, and disposal information for each demonstration whenever the audience is encouraged to repeat the demonstration.

12. Arrange for appropriate waste containers for and subsequent disposal of materials harmful to the environment.

Background for Teachers

This section provides you, the teacher, with a brief overview of the polymer industry, a summary of Quantum Chemical Corporation's role in this industry, and a content review.

Overview of the Polymer Industry

Plastics and polymers are all around us. Today more than 90% of all products contain polymers. Included in this list are milk jugs, sandwich bags, disposable diapers, adhesive bandages, zippers, car-battery cases, wire insulation, and auto parts. While synthetic polymers are a relatively recent discovery, some natural polymers have been used for thousands of years. For example, traces of shellac have been found as far back as early Egyptian and Roman cultures. Other natural polymers such as wool, cotton, silk, and flax fibers have also been around for thousands of years. Synthetic polymers such as nylon, polyethylene, and polystyrene have only come to the forefront of chemistry in the past one hundred years or so.

A milestone in the development of plastic occurred in 1907 when Leo Baekeland prepared the first completely synthetic plastic, called Bakelite®. Bakelite was made by reacting phenol and formaldehyde in the presence of acid or base. This hard, dark-colored material was initially used for the production of radio sets and electrical plugs. Urea-formaldehyde polymers were first developed in the 1920s and are commonly used today as resins for particle board manufacturing and as foams for insulation.

Although many new polymers were being developed during the 1920s and 1930s, the molecular nature of polymers was unknown until the work of Wallace Carothers at DuPont. Using the fundamental knowledge that polymers were high-molecular-weight compounds of repeating units, Carothers first synthesized the polyamide, nylon, in 1938.

Other synthetic polymers quickly followed. Polyethylene, developed in Britain in 1939 by Imperial Chemical Industries (ICI), was used in radar equipment during World War II. Another important polymer was styrene-butadiene rubber (SBR). This polymer was synthesized for use as a replacement for natural rubber during World War II. Charles Goodyear produced vulcanized rubber (the hard form of rubber used in tires) by crosslinking (or joining) the polymer chains using sulfur atoms. Today, a variety of synthetic polymers such as polymethyl methacrylate (Plexiglas®), polyethylene terephthalate (PET or PETE), and polyvinyl chloride (PVC) are commonly used. These synthetic polymers are usually called plastics.

All synthetic organic polymers are made from oil, natural gas, or coal products. Of the many chemicals produced from these raw materials, ethylene is probably the most important because it is the starting material for many kinds of polymers, as shown in Figure 1.

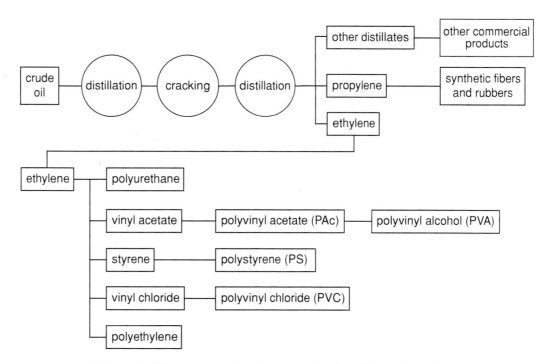

Figure 1: The progression from crude oil to its end products

As the use of plastics in disposable items has increased, plastics have developed a negative reputation regarding their disposal. However, detailed investigations indicate that plastics account for only 21% by volume (8% by weight) of municipal solid waste, while paper and cardboard make up 32% of such waste, according to the American Plastics Council. Most of the plastics in landfills are polyethylene and polystyrene. These polymers are inert (won't decompose) and are unaffected by rain or chemicals in the air or soil. This minimizes pollution of the soil or groundwater. However, these inert polymers remain intact in a landfill for a long time.

Biodegradable plastics are usually combinations of plastic and a degradable material such as cellulose or starch. Degradation takes place when the starch breaks down and the plastic between the starch molecules comes apart leaving minute pieces of plastic once this process is complete. However, for biodegradable plastics to break down, water and oxygen must be present. In a modern, well-run landfill, both are minimized to prevent leaching, pollution, odors, and bacterial growth. In order to reduce the amount of plastics sent to landfills, today's plastics industry is concerned with resource conservation, including source reduction and recovery through recycling, reuse, and energy recapture. One alternative to putting plastics in a landfill is to use them as fuel—plastics generate large amounts of heat during incineration.

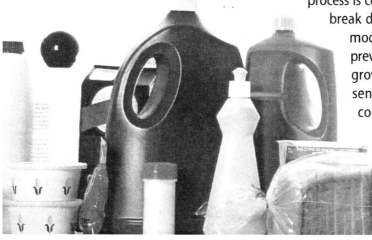

Plastic products come in all shapes and sizes.

Quantum Chemical Corporation, a wholly-owned operating unit of Hanson PLC, is headquartered in Cincinnati, Ohio. Founded in 1906, Quantum Chemical Corporation has taken advantage of technological developments to produce major new products with broad market potential, but always based upon its original expertise in hydrocarbon synthesis. Industrial-grade ethyl alcohol for the pharmaceutical, personal care, and chemical industries was Quantum's first product in 1906. In the early 1950s, Quantum moved into production of polyethylene plastic with its extensive consumer and industrial markets. By the late 1980s, through purchases and acquisitions, Quantum was the largest domestic producer of polyethylene, as well as a major manufacturer of polypropylene and a number of specialty polymers.

In 1993, Quantum was acquired by Hanson PLC, a major British-American company. Headquartered in London, Hanson has interests in the chemical, forest products, coal, aggregates, construction, and propane marketing industries.

Today, Quantum is still the largest domestic producer of polyethylene, which is the largest volume plastic sold in the country. The company also manufactures polypropylene, ethylene vinyl acetate copolymers, colorants and additives for plastics, wire and cable resins and compounds, specialty polymers, industrial ethyl alcohol, ethyl ether, methanol, acetic acid, and vinyl acetate monomer. See Table 1 for general descriptions of common items made from Quantum products.

Table 1: Examples of Products Manufactured from Quantum Products

Polymer Type	Examples of Products
low-density polyethylene	toys, bottle caps, housewares, garments, produce and food-storage bags, coatings for frozen-food boxes and milk cartons, insulation and jacketing for wire
linear low-density polyethylene	trash and merchandise bags, large hollow containers and bins, housewares, traffic-control devices, wire and cable applications
high-density polyethylene	plastic bottles for liquid food, household chemicals, and personal care products; molded furniture; toys; housewares; automotive parts; wire and cable applications
polypropylene	automotive parts, auto-battery cases, luggage, caps and closures, child-safety seats
ethylene vinyl acetate copolymers	flexible and rigid packaging for low-temperature applications, adhesives, sealants, and coatings

In 1992, Quantum responded to growing public and industry concern over solid waste issues by opening the Heath Recycling Plant. This plant is capable of producing 32 million pounds per year of post-consumer high-density polyethylene resin. Feed materials for this recycling process, mostly baled plastic milk bottles and mixed colored plastic bottles, are sold to the Heath Recycling Plant from as far as 1,000 miles away. The plastic resins produced at Heath are used by plastic processors to manufacture new bottles for non-food items, fiberfill, film, plastic "lumber," and other materials.

Quantum's Allen Research Center and Process Research Center

Nearly 200 research scientists and engineers are employed at the Allen Research Center in Cincinnati and at Quantum's Process Research Center in Morris, Illinois. The Process Research Center is adjacent to one of the company's large polymer production plants.

Research and development at Quantum Chemical Corporation is a dynamic process focused on all aspects of the continuum from scientific conceptualization through pilot plant scale-up to customer end-use. Research and development's mission is technology leadership. Efforts to achieve and sustain this mission are focused in two departments: Polyethylene Research and Development; and Chemicals, Specialties and Exploratory Research and Development.

Chemicals, Specialties and Exploratory Research and Development, located at the Allen Research Center, investigates catalysts used in the synthesis of commodity chemicals, new polymers and compounds for the development of specialty polymers and composites, and the molecular structure and properties of polymers to permit the optimal development of new products. Some major areas of interest are sophisticated analytical studies, polymer rheology research, polymer chemistry, polymer physics, and exploratory catalysis research.

Polyethylene Research and Development, located at both the Allen Research Center and at the Process Research Center in Morris, Illinois, focuses on the science and technology associated with Quantum's polyethylene business. Promising new catalysts are scaled up and evaluated at the Process Research Center with its five state-of-the-art pilot plant facilities. These polymers are subsequently tested in the Applications Laboratory. In addition, this group provides technical service support to customers, either at the customer's own plant or in the Applications Laboratory.

Quantum Chemical Corporation Headquarters in Cincinnati, Ohio

Content Review

This section provides a basic overview of some of the more important and complex content areas to be addressed in the activities.

Carbon Bonding

Most polymers are organic (carbon-containing). Carbon is the basic atom in all organic molecules, including coal, oil, and their by-products, which are starting materials for most polymers. An exceptionally large number of different carbon compounds exist or can be made, largely because of carbon's ability to bond to other carbon atoms to form exceptionally long chains.

Carbon is a tetravalent atom; that is, it has four electrons that are available for bonding with other atoms such as other carbons (C), hydrogen (H), oxygen (O), nitrogen (N), etc. Carbon can form these four bonds in a number of different ways. For example, carbon can make single bonds to as many as four other atoms. (See Figure 2.)

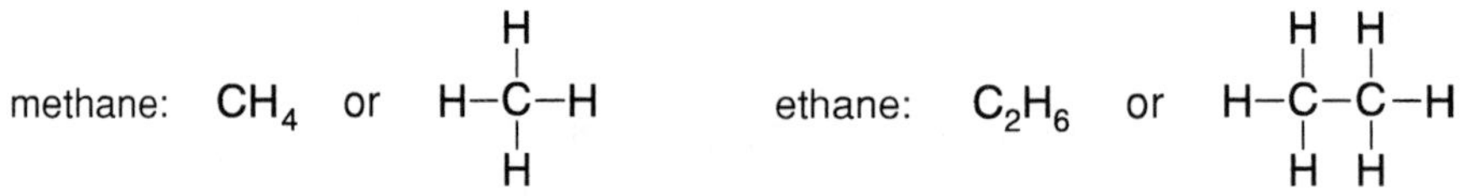

methane: CH_4 or H—C—H (with H above and H below)   ethane: C_2H_6 or H—C—C—H (with H above and below each C)

Figure 2: Carbon can form single bonds.

Sometimes carbon will form two bonds (a double bond) to another carbon atom or to an atom like oxygen. (See Figure 3.)

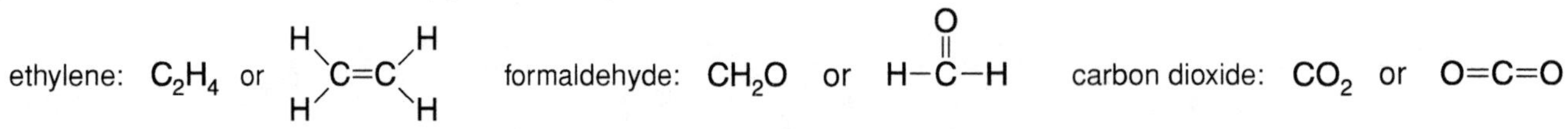

ethylene: C_2H_4 or H₂C=CH₂   formaldehyde: CH_2O or H—C—H (with O double bonded above)   carbon dioxide: CO_2 or O=C=O

Figure 3: Carbon can form double bonds.

Carbon can also form three bonds (a triple bond) with another carbon atom or another element like nitrogen. (See Figure 4.)

ethyne: C_2H_2 or H—C≡C—H   hydrogen cyanide: HCN or H—C≡N

Figure 4: Carbon can form triple bonds.

The types of bonding that exist in organic compounds are very important when forming polymers.

Polymers from Monomers

Polymers are defined as long chains of simple molecules called monomers. Basically, all polymers are giant molecules, or macromolecules, with anywhere from 1,000 to 50,000 monomers linked together. The monomers that make up a polymer may be identical or different. The conditions needed to join the monomers together may include high pressure, high temperature, and/or the presence of a catalyst. Under the proper conditions, these monomers can be joined to form long-chain polymers (linear polymers), chains with branches (branched polymers), and even multi-branched polymers (network polymers).

Different types of polymers have diverse properties. Some polymers are very hard and rigid while others are soft and flexible. Some polymers are resistant to heat while others melt easily. Some polymers can be molded and shaped into useful objects while others resist deformation, even at high pressures and temperatures. These properties depend on many factors such as the type of monomer, molecular weight, molecular weight distribution, the amount of branching, the strength of the intermolecular forces between the polymer chains (e.g., hydrogen bonds and van der Waals forces), and the regularity and flexibility of the polymer chain itself. Scientists can control and determine the properties of a given polymer by controlling these various factors during production. Table 2 lists some common polymers along with their properties and uses.

Table 2: Some Common Polymers

Polymer	Monomer Unit	Properties	Polymer Uses
polyethylene	$-CH_2-CH_2-$	lightweight, tough, flexible; resistant to water, frost, electricity, and chemicals; easily colored and molded; inexpensive to produce	low-density: bowls, buckets, beakers, toys, squeeze bottles and tubes, stoppers for bottles, piping, power and telephone cable, packaging, and disposal bags linear-low-density: trash and merchandise bags, large hollow containers, housewares, traffic control devices, wire and cable applications
polypropylene	$-CH_2-CH-$ with CH_3 branch	similar to polyethylene except more rigid and more heat-resistant	hospital and lab equipment that needs to be sterilized, baler twine and rope, chair seats, tool handles, shoe heels, toys
polyvinyl chloride	$-CH_2-CH-$ with Cl branch	strong, water- and weatherproof, durable	pipes for chemical plants, water, gutters, and soil; boots and casual shoes; washable vinyl wallpaper; tablecloths; shower curtains; baby pants; inflatable toys and squeaky dolls; floor tiles
polystyrene	$-CH_2-CH-$ with phenyl ring branch	crystal clear but brittle; if stretched becomes opaque; good insulator; resistant to water and acid	clear storage containers, reels and spools for film or tape, yogurt containers, disposable cups, refrigerator linings and trays, TV and radio cabinets, pen barrels expanded polystyrene: ceiling tiles, insulation, meat and food trays, packaging
acrylic (polymethyl methacrylate)	$-CH_2-C-$ with CH_3 branch and $-C(=O)-O-CH_3$ branch	hard, transparent, can be colored, weatherproof, lightweight, easily molded	replaces glass where unbreakable or curved window is required, watch glasses, contact lenses, false teeth, goggles, safety guards on machines, street light covers, car rear lights
nylon	$-N(CH_2)_6N-C(CH_2)_8C-$ with H, H, O, O substituents	very tough and rigid; resistant to water, corrosion, wear, and high temperatures	solid: used in gears, bearing parts, curtain runners thick thread: fishing nets, tennis racket strings, ropes, and carpets thinner thread: bristle for brushes, fishing lines fine thread: used widely in textile industry
polyester	$-O-(CH_2)_2-O-C-$ (phenyl ring) $-C-$ with O, O	does not stretch; keeps shape well; brittle but, in combination with glass fibers, very strong	transparent roasting bags, magnetic tape, glass fiber reinforcement for boat hulls, some car bodies, some roofing panels, resistant finish for furniture against chemicals and heat
polyurethane	$-O-(CH_2)_n-O-C-N-(CH_2)_m-N-C-$ with O, H, H, O	rigid foam: heat insulator, water-resistant flexible foam: sound absorber, insulator	surface coating for furniture and floors, foams used to form to furniture before covering or shipping, machine parts, stools, bowls, weatherproof sealing strips

Polyethylene

Ethylene, the monomer from which polyethylene is made, is produced in the cracking of petroleum distillates. In this process, the mixture of hydrocarbons (usually molecules between 5–9 carbons in length) is broken down into shorter carbon-carbon chains. When hydrogen atoms are removed through a dehydrogenation reaction, the resulting hydrocarbons become unsaturated. (Carbon-carbon double bonds are formed.) Ethylene is the simplest of these unsaturated hydrocarbons. (See Figure 5.)

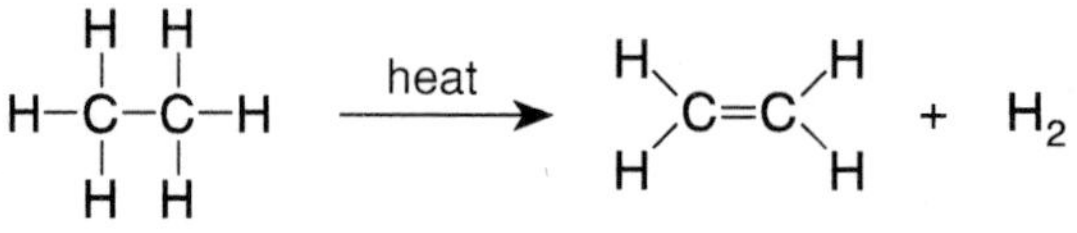

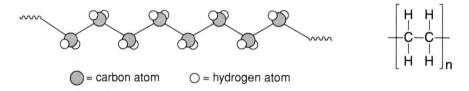

Figure 5: The dehydrogenation of ethane into ethylene

Polyethylene is formed by the covalent bonding of many monomers of ethylene molecules ($H_2C=CH_2$). Under the right conditions, the double bond between the two carbon atoms can break open, forming a reactive intermediate capable of bonding with other molecules. If it reacts with other ethylene molecules, a long chain of repeating ethylene molecules will be formed that is quite stable. Because of the way it is formed, this polymer is called polyethylene (meaning many ethylene molecules). Figure 6 shows a short segment of the polyethylene molecule as a ball-and-stick model and in shorthand notation. The carbons form a zigzag chain with the hydrogen atoms projecting off the carbons. Polyethylene chains can be rather short or enormously long, consisting of many thousands of atoms.

⬤ = carbon atom   ◯ = hydrogen atom

Figure 6: A segment of a polyethylene molecule and the shorthand notation

Polyethylene (PE) has become the world's largest volume plastic, with the U.S. production alone being about 15 billion pounds a year. It has a range of densities from 0.91–0.97 g/cm³. A classification dividing polyethylene resins into four ranges of density is generally accepted in the industry. Table 3 shows that even an item made of the highest density polyethylene will float on water.

Table 3: The Four Density Ranges of Polyethylene

Density	g/cm³
low	0.910 to 0.925
medium	0.926 to 0.940
high (linear)	0.941 to 0.959
very high	0.960 and above

Polyethylene is a tough material unlikely to break in many of its applications. Although it can be colored, PE itself is opaque white, but when extruded into film, it can range from translucent to crystal clear. PE can be a soft, tough, flexible material with high impact strength, or hard and rigid but still tough. It does not become brittle until cooled to –100°C, and it melts between 100°C and 137°C.

Different forms of the polymer are possible depending on the degree of branching in its structure. Low-density polyethylene (LDPE) is a branched polymer whose branches interfere with chain packing. (See Figure 7.) This accounts for the low density and a comparatively high degree of amorphous (random) character. High-density polyethylene (HDPE) has less branching and more regular packing, leading to high crystallinity and higher density.

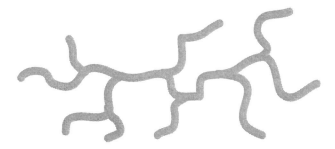

Figure 7: Diagram of a branched polymer

The major use of branched low-density PE is in products such as films used in frozen-food packaging, ice bags, shrink wrapping, meat packaging, other product wrapping, and flexible bottles. The linear high-density PE is used in more rigid containers such as milk bottles, bleach bottles, detergent and antifreeze containers, storage tanks, and drums.

Types of Polymerization Reactions

Polyethylene is an example of an addition polymerization reaction. Addition polymerization has several general characteristics:

- The chain reaction occurs very rapidly (less than 0.1 second).

- Very little initiator is needed. (An initiator is a molecule that starts the polymerization reaction.)

- The polymerization process is usually exothermic. (Heat is released.)

- The polymer products have high molecular weights (10,000–10,000,000 amu).

- Branching and crosslinking occur frequently.

In the case of ethylene, polymerization proceeds as shown in Figure 8. R• represents the initiator which attacks the double bond, breaks it open, and begins the polymerization process. This process continues until there are no more monomers to react or some sort of molecule quenches (stops) the reaction.

Figure 8 shows a reaction proceeding with the help of a catalyst. A catalyst is a substance that affects the rate of a chemical reaction without being consumed. If easily recovered from the reaction, catalysts can be used over and over again. A small quantity of catalyst should affect the rate of reaction for a large amount of reactant. In addition, the presence of a catalyst will not change the equilibrium constant for the reaction. Catalysts provide a new mechanism for a reaction by lowering the activation energy for the reactants to be converted to products. This means that a larger proportion of the collisions between the reactants now have enough energy to overcome the activation barrier and form products.

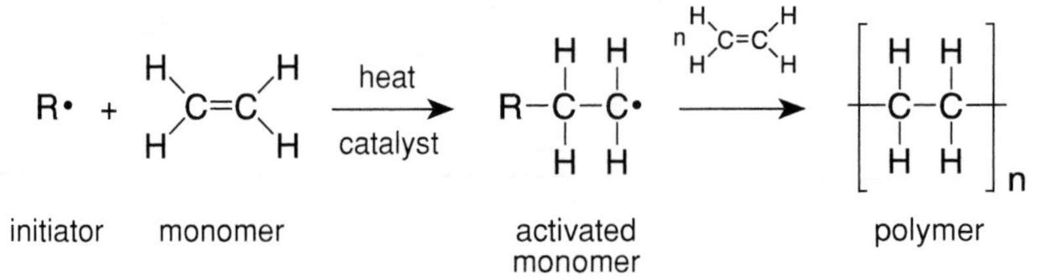

Figure 8: Polymerization of ethylene

The second type of polymerization reaction is condensation polymerization. Condensation polymerization has several general characteristics:

- The polymerization does not involve an initiator.

- The monomers are difunctional, meaning that they have a chemically active group at each end of the molecule.

- As the monomers are linked together, a small molecule, such as water, is released.

- The extent of the polymerization is dependent on the mobility of the ends of the growing polymer.

- Removal of the small molecule produced by the reaction is essential for driving the reaction to completion.

Nylon is an example of a polyamide. Polyesters and polyurethanes are also condensation polymers. In the case of nylon 6-6, the polymerization proceeds as shown in Figure 9. Note that each monomer is difunctional: adipic acid contains a carboxylic acid group on each end of the molecule; hexamethylenediamine contains an amine group on each of its ends. Nylon 6-6 can be extended indefinitely as long as both monomers are available. The resulting polymer will not have branches because each of the functional groups (the acid and the amine group) is used just to keep the polymer chain growing linearly.

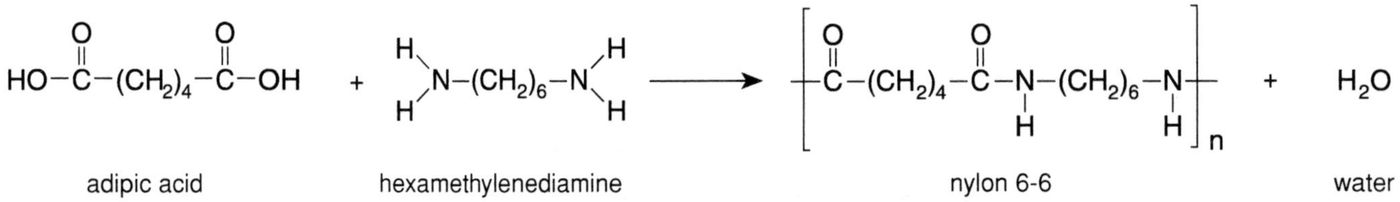

Figure 9: The polymerization of nylon 6-6

Some Interesting Characteristics of Polymers

Bonding. Since most polymers are carbon compounds, the primary bonding is covalent, which lends strength to the individual molecules. Secondary interactions that occur between polymer molecules include hydrogen bonds, dipole interaction, van der Waals forces, and ionic bonds. The type of bonding in an individual polymer helps account for its properties.

While some polymers naturally exist in the liquid state at room temperature, they can often be made more solid or gel-like by the addition of a crosslinker. A crosslinker is a small molecule or ion which bonds to two different polymer strands and thus restricts the movement of the individual polymer strands. This causes the characteristics of the polymer to become more gel-like and less fluid. For example, aqueous solutions of polyvinyl alcohol or guar gum, when crosslinked, become quite gel-like and take on the consistency of Slime®, a common toy.

Effects of Heat. Another interesting characteristic of polymers is their response to heat. Synthetic polymers can be divided into two groups: thermoplastics and thermosets. Thermoplastic polymers can be heated until molten, molded, and cooled to fix the shape. The advantage of a thermoplastic is that it can be heated again, molded, and fixed into a new shape. This process has the potential of being repeated any number of times. Polyethylene behaves in this manner, becoming pliable when heated but hardening when cooled down again.

Unlike thermoplastics, thermoset polymers have crosslinks between the polymer chains which form when the polymer is first heated. These links become permanent once the polymer is set, making the polymer resistant to change with heat. Products formed from thermoset polymers retain their shape and are heat-resistant. This process is much like that of frying an egg. The action of the heat transforms the egg from its original form in the shell to a new form which is permanent. Like the egg, thermoset plastics are capable of charring and decomposing if the temperature becomes high enough. The plastic handles used on pots and pans are made from thermoset polymers.

Molecular Weight. The molecular weight of a polymer is an important factor in determining its properties. Molecular weights are calculated by adding up the individual atomic weights of all the atoms in the molecule. This process is easy as long as the formula of the compound is known, but in polymers like polyethylene, the formulas can be expressed as $(-CH_2-CH_2-)_n$. How big is n? Determining the molecular weight of a polymer is extremely important in characterizing a polymer. The strength of a polymer, its solubility, elasticity, absorption on solids, and tear strength all depend on the molecular weight. For example, a minimum molecular weight of 10,000 amu is necessary for significant strength. Strength increases up to a molecular weight of 50,000 to 100,000 amu. Beyond this molecular weight, the increase in strength slows and finally levels off. For a discussion about the methodologies involved in molecular weight determination, see the Determination of Average Molecular Weight subsection.

Average molecular weights can be used to characterize a polymer sample. Generally, polyethylenes most suitable for applications such as film extrusion or blow molding should have average molecular weights in a range somewhat higher than for some other applications such as injection molding. Extrusion and molding applications are discussed in more detail in the Polymer Manufacturing Techniques section.

Molecular Weight Distribution. For some polymers, the molecular weight distribution (MWD) gives a general picture of the ratio of the large, medium, and small molecular chains in the polymer. The MWD is called narrow if the polymer is made up of chains close to the average length; it is called wide if the polymer is made up of chains of a wide variety of lengths. Figure 10 shows this in graph form.

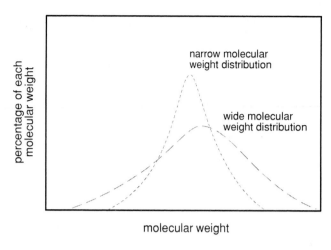

Figure 10: Schematic representation of molecular weight distribution

Actual molecular weight distribution curves often vary considerably from the shapes of those in Figure 10. Recent work has shown that the shape of the curves may be just as important as the overall distribution. For this reason, it is difficult to make simple correlations between molecular weight distribution and polymer physical properties. Work is continuing in this area of polymer research.

How Density and Molecular Weight Affect Essential Polymer Properties. Table 4 shows how density and molecular weight affect essential properties of polyethylene. There are some properties which are definitely not influenced by either of these basic molecular factors, but depend on other peculiar traits of the molecular structure such as molecular weight distribution or configuration; and there are others for which such influence may be proved at a later date.

As Table 4 shows, the two basic molecular properties may have contrary effects on certain polymer or end product properties. In such cases, the end use will determine which properties are most essential and which polyethylene is best suited for a particular end use.

With increasing density, such important properties as the heat-softening point, resistance to gas and moisture vapor permeation, film clarity (both transparency and freedom from haze), and gloss are improved, though at some sacrifice of other properties such as flexibility and film impact strength. Such a combination of properties may be favorable for making some kinds of bags or for blow molding. It may be less favorable for such articles as heavy-duty fruit or vegetable bags.

An increase in the average molecular weight may make the polyethylene more suitable for specific packaging applications which require toughness. An item made of a higher-molecular-weight polyethylene resin also has better resistance to environmental stress cracking, that is, to cracking when subjected to stresses in the presence of such liquids as household detergents, oils, or solvents.

Thus, higher-molecular-weight polyethylene polymers are made into carboys used as shipping containers for acids or into squeeze bottles. Since viscosity (resistance to flow) when molten increases with molecular weight, higher-molecular-weight polyethylene becomes more difficult to extrude and requires higher extrusion temperatures. On the other hand, polyethylene of lower molecular weight is used for such applications as injection molding at low temperatures and fast cycle times. Whenever higher output is desired and some other properties are not necessary, lower-molecular-weight polyethylene is useful.

Table 4: Some Generalized Effects of Changes in Density and Molecular Weight on Polyethylene Properties*

Physical Property	Molecular Properties	
	If Density Increases	**If Average Molecular Weight Decreases**
melt viscosity	—	lower
vicat softening temperature	much higher	lower
surface hardening (abrasion resistance)	higher	slightly lower
tensile strength:		
• yield	much higher	slightly lower
• break	slightly lower	lower
• elongation	lower	lower
• resistance to creep	higher	slightly lower
flexural stiffness	much higher	slightly lower
flexibility	lower	—
resistance to brittleness at low temperatures	lower	lower
resistance to environmental stress cracking	lower	lower
barrier properties:		
• MVT rate	lower	—
• gas and liquid transmission	much lower	—
• grease resistance	much higher	slightly lower
• adhesion to surfaces	slightly lower	slightly higher
• shrinkage	higher	lower
• warpage	slightly higher	lower
• electrical properties	slightly higher	no effect

*The relationships between these two basic molecular properties and the physical and other properties of polyethylene are not always simple and clear. Often, molecular features exert some influence on certain physical properties. Processing conditions may radically change the orientation (alignment) of the molecules in the resin and thus also affect some of its properties. High-density polyethylene resins do not always exhibit the same degree of property change with density change that low-density resins do. For these reasons, this table should be considered only a starting point for a generalized discussion.

Determination of Average Molecular Weight. The characterizations of different polymer samples typically include details on the average molecular weight of the sample. Several different methods can be used to determine average molecular weight—each has its own limitations and usefulness.

Commonly used methods to determine molecular weight include determination of freezing-point depression, boiling-point elevation, vapor pressure, or osmotic pressure of the sample. Of these four methods, osmotic pressure is used most frequently. This method is usually limited to polymers with molecular weights of 50,000–1,000,000.

Another method, light scattering, uses a laser to determine molecular weight. In light scattering experiments, the intensity of light scattered is directly proportional to the molecular weight. The intensity of light scattered increases with molecular weight, and is used on polymers with molecular weights of 10,000–10,000,000. The upper limit on the molecular weight that can be determined is set by the solubility of the polymer in the solvent.

A third way to determine molecular weight is using the polymer's viscosity. Viscosity is a measure of the resistance to flow. Large molecules tend to impede flow and have a high viscosity. A molecule of a polymer moves with the same average velocity as the liquid in which it is dissolved, but the great length of the molecule reduces the velocity of the solvent by restricting its free flow. The larger the molecule, the greater the effect. This technique can give a good approximation of the average molecular weight of the polymer.

A fourth way to determine molecular weight involves an analytical technique called chromatography. Liquid chromatography is an important technique used for the molecular weight determination of polymers as well as the detection of impurities or additives in polymers. A mobile phase is continually pumped through a column packed with particles. Sample components are separated based on their different interactions with the stationary phase. As the separated components come off the column, they are detected, often by a UV-VIS or refractive index detector. A different chromatography technique, gel permeation chromatography (GPC), can be used to separate polymers of different molecular weights. In this method, separation depends on how easily the components can penetrate the pores of the column packing. The movement of small components is retarded, while larger components come off the column easily.

Melt Index and Melt Viscosity. The melt index is an important characteristic of polyethylene that is largely, though not exclusively, dependent upon the average molecular weight. Generally, polyethylene of high molecular weight has a low melt index, and vice versa.

Melt index describes the flow behavior of polyethylene at a specified temperature and under a specified pressure. With the aid of an apparatus called a melt indexer, the weight of melted polyethylene which a weighted piston extrudes through an orifice in a specified period of time is measured. During the measurement, the temperature is held at 190°C (374°F). The melt index of the polymer sample is the weight, in grams, extruded in 10 minutes. If the melt index of a polymer is low, its melt viscosity or melt-flow resistance is high, and vice versa. Melt-flow resistance is the resistance of the molten plastic to flow when making film, pipe, or containers. Thus, polymers with a higher melt index generally flow more easily in the hot, molten state than those with a lower melt index.

To the processor, melt viscosity is an extremely important property because all of the processing operations involve melting the plastic and then moving it to fill a given cavity, such as a mold, or to form it to a given shape through a die.

Non-Newtonian Fluids. Non-Newtonian fluids can act like fluids, but do not obey all the rules that common fluids, such as water, do. For example, these polymers will flow (slowly) if left undisturbed. With gentle pressure they can be shaped like clay. Under intense pressure (like that caused by hitting the floor at high speed) they will become rigid. In the case of a ball shaped from a non-Newtonian fluid, the impact energy of the ball hitting the floor is not absorbed in permanently deforming the ball. Instead, much of it remains as mechanical energy and is used to make the ball bounce high. It is this peculiar characteristic of some polymers that results, for example, in a silicone polymer super ball with the characteristics of both a clay ball and a Ping-Pong™ ball. Some organic polymers also show characteristics of non-Newtonian fluids. "Slime" and Corn Starch Putty are examples of non-Newtonian fluids.

Polymer Manufacturing Techniques

Most polymers exit the reactor as a powder which is made into pellets for ease of handling. These pellets are fashioned by heating up the powder, extruding it, and then chopping it into strands. Manufacturers warm the pellets until they are liquid and then apply various techniques to the liquid polymers to shape them into different end products.

Compression Molding. One technique used to manufacture polymer items is called compression molding. Compression molding involves placing some of the polymer into a mold shape and then applying pressure and heat to set the polymer. The objects are then cooled before removing them from the molds.

Injection Molding. The most common method of manufacturing plastic products is called injection molding. Injection molding involves heating the polymer, injecting it under pressure into a cold mold, where it cools and hardens, and then releasing the mold to remove the plastic article. The articles made using this technique come off the production line with a small bump where they were cut off at the nozzle. Although the bump is cut level, it is always present, especially on objects like plastic bowls.

Blow Molding. Another common method used to manufacture plastic products is called blow molding. In this process, the heated plastic is extruded in the form of tubes. The mold is in two halves which close, fitting around the polymer tube and sealing off one end. Air, under pressure, is blown into the open end of the mold, and the tube is blown up until it takes the shape of the mold. This technique leaves a slight ridge or seam around the article where the two halves of the mold met. Blow molding is most often used to produce bottles.

Extrusion. Extrusion is the process of applying heat and pressure to melt a polymer and force it through an accurately dimensioned hole (die). The shape of the final product is determined by the shape of the die at the end of the extruder. This process can be used to continuously produce shapes in the form of unsupported film and sheeting; pipe and other profiles; film for coating paper, paper board, metal foil, cloth, plastics, and other substrates; or coating around wire or cable.

Vacuum Molding. Another technique involves clamping plastic sheets into a frame over a mold and heating it. When the plastic is flexible, it is suddenly sucked down onto the mold where it cools, taking on the complicated shape of the mold. This process is called vacuum molding and is ideal for creating the plastic trays for chocolates or egg cartons.

Rotational Molding. Rotational molding is a process by which a powdered polymer is placed into a mold, and the mold is heated and then rotated in three dimensions so that a layer of plastic covers the walls of the mold. This process is ideal for producing large, hollow parts such as storage tanks.

Dip Coating. To cover objects with a layer of plastic, a technique called dip coating can be employed. Examples of objects that are dip-coated would be plastic-coated metal dish racks, gloves, and some Wellington boots. The thickness of the plastic layer depends on the temperature of the dipping bath.

Laminating. Laminating is another technique in which layers of cloth or soaked paper and plastics are pressed between two heated molds and then cooled to form a board. Sometimes metal is laminated with plastics for use in electronics.

Polymer Recycling Codes

For plastics to be recycled, they must be separated by type. The polymer recycling codes shown in Table 5 enable us to distinguish between the six types of polymers typically used in making bottles and other containers. Each code includes a unique number in the center and distinguishing letters under the triangle. The codes are molded or imprinted on the bottom of most plastic containers. This coding system and the manual sorting that goes with it are interim solutions until more automated systems have been perfected.

Table 5: Polymer Recycling Codes and Uses

Recycling Symbol	Name of Polymer	Sample Uses
♳ 1 PETE	polyethylene terephthalate	• soft drink bottles • carpets • fiberfill • rope • scouring pads • fabrics • Mylar tape (cassette and computer)
♴ 2 HDPE	high density polyethylene	• milk jugs • detergent bottles • bags • plastic lumber • garden furniture • flowerpots • trash cans • signs
♵ 3 V	vinyl	• cooking oil bottles • drainage and sewer pipes • tile • bird feeders • institutional furniture • credit cards
♶ 4 LDPE	low density polyethylene	• bags • Elmer's® glue bottles and other squeeze bottles • wrapping films • container lids
♷ 5 PP	polypropylene	• yogurt containers • automobile batteries • bottles • lab equipment • carpets • rope • wrapping films
♸ 6 PS	polystyrene	• disposable cups and utensils • toys • lighting and signs • construction • foam containers and insulation
♹ 7 other	all other polymers	• catsup, snack and other food containers • hand cream, toothpaste, and cosmetic containers

Using the Activities in the Classroom

The activities in this module will help students to become aware of the uses and benefits of polymers in virtually every aspect of their lives. They will also become aware of the roles technology and industry have played in the history and development of our modern society.

Pedagogical Strategies

Since students are familiar with the term "plastic," teachers may want to introduce this unit by challenging students to define the term and give examples of common plastics. The discussion can then extend to the following characteristics of plastics; they

- are synthetic,

- are moldable (have the ability to be shaped under the action of heat and/or force),

- have solid and liquid characteristics,

- are made from petroleum products such as oil and natural gas, and

- are polymers.

The transition can then be made to polymers, their properties, and their preparation. The following sections provide some suggestions on how this can be effectively accomplished.

Kinesthetic Demonstrations and Simulations

Kinesthetic demonstrations, which involve students in role playing and dramatic simulations, can be can be useful in providing an understanding of the nature of polymer chains.

Repeating Units. The repeating unit characteristic of polymers can be shown by having several students hold hands or link arms to form a long chain. (If students are opposed to holding hands, you can have each student grasp one end of a pipe cleaner or pencil or try linking arms.) Define each student as a monomer (mono = one and mer = unit). Each link in the chain represents a chemical bond. The chain that the students have formed simulates a polymer (poly = many and mer = unit). You may want to emphasize that polymers typically include hundreds or thousands of repeating units. To show the class how flexible the polymer chain is when in the liquid state, lead the chain around the room, weaving between the desks and chairs.

The nature and flexibility of polymer chains can be similarly demonstrated by creating long chains of paper clips and "pop beads" or "pop toys." Figure 11a represents a segment of a polymer chain made of single monomer units. By using two different-colored, different-shaped, or different-sized clips or beads, the types of copolymers can be illustrated. The regular, repeating pattern of alternating monomers is shown in Figure 11b. Copolymers can also have a random orientation as shown in Figure 11c. The third type of copolymer is a block polymer which is represented in Figure 11d.

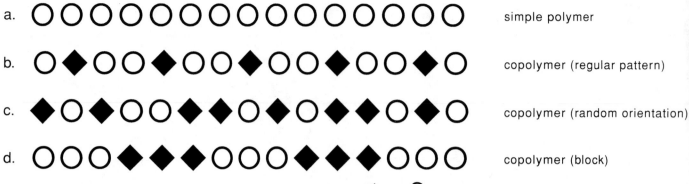

a.	○○○○○○○○○○○○○○	simple polymer
b.	○◆○○◆○○◆○○◆○○◆○	copolymer (regular pattern)
c.	◆○◆○○◆◆○◆○◆◆○◆○	copolymer (random orientation)
d.	○○○◆◆◆○○○◆◆◆○○○	copolymer (block)

Figure 11: Representations of polymer chains with ◆ and ○ being different monomers

The exceptional length of a polymer chain compared to its thickness can be dramatically illustrated by forming a "pop bead" chain of 4,000 beads to simulate the typical polyethylene chain. By carefully arranging the chain in a bucket, it can be made to siphon out of the bucket by hanging one end over the side and holding the container well above the floor or table. The sight and sound of beads siphoning from the bucket and the time it takes for all the beads to appear keeps the attention of the audience.

Synthesis Dramatizations. The synthesis of both addition and condensation polymers can be dramatized by the following kinesthetic demonstrations. Polyethylene is an addition polymer. It is made from the ethylene monomer ($CH_2=CH_2$) simulated in this demonstration by three or four pairs of students facing each other and holding hands. The grasped hands represent the double bond in the ethylene molecule. The students can wear head bands with two springs attached available at toy or party supply stores. On the ends of the springs, attach cards with an H printed on them to represent the two hydrogens on each carbon atom. Explain that the ethylene monomers are very content (stable) as they are. They do not polymerize by themselves.

Ethylene is a gas and its molecules are actually moving around and colliding with each other and the walls of the container. In spite of this, the polymerization process does not occur until it is initiated by a special molecule called a free radical. The teacher wearing a clown wig and a "radical" shirt can come out with one hand behind his/her back. The free hand represents an unpaired electron which makes the free radical a very reactive species. This free radical goes looking for electrons to pair with. Remind the students that the electron-rich part of the ethylene molecule is the double bond. Ask the students where they think the free radical will attack. As the free radical attacks the double bond, the teacher takes the hand of one of the students in one of the pairs. In doing so, the other student is left with one free hand and a new, larger free radical is made. This new free radical is also electron deficient and goes looking for another double bond. As the free radical encounters double bonds, the process repeats and the chain grows. (See Figure 12.) This is how addition polymers are synthesized. The polymerization process (hooking ethylene molecules together) continues until there are no more molecules to accept the free radical, until two free radicals combine, or until some other quencher is added.

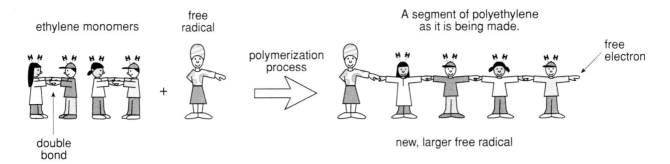

ethylene monomers | free radical | polymerization process | A segment of polyethylene as it is being made. | free electron

double bond

new, larger free radical

Figure 12: Kinesthetic demonstration of the synthesis of an addition polymer

Condensation polymerization is similar to the addition polymerization process except that when the two monomers are hooked together, a small molecule, like water or carbon dioxide, is formed. This can be demonstrated using six students, three students wearing gloves on each of their hands and three students wearing mittens. Simulate the reaction by linking a gloved hand and a mittened hand; as they link hands, have each student remove the glove or mitten from his or her hand. Roll the glove and mitten together like a pair of socks and drop them on the floor, then join the free hands to form a bond. This process continues with one glove from the chain joining with a mitten from an unreacted monomer, the glove-mitten falling on the floor, and the free hands joining to form a bond. The release of the glove-mitten unit represents the small molecule that is formed when the two monomers are bonded together. This polymerization process continues as long as there are unreacted monomer units. The preparation of Nylon 6-10 (Activity 7) involves a condensation polymerization process with hydrochloric acid lost as the small molecule.

Crosslinked Dramatizations. The "Glue Polymer" (Activity 14), "Making a Super Ball" (Activity 16), and "Homemade Slimes" (Activity 15) all involve the crosslinking of existing polymers. Crosslinking greatly affects the flow properties of the polymer. The nature of polymer chains can be shown through this simple kinesthetic activity. Have 4–5 students stand in a line facing the class. Tell the class that each of these students represents a monomer. Have the monomers link arms or hold hands. Each pair of clasped hands represents a chemical bond. The chain they form is made of many units, simulating a polymer chain. Emphasize that polymers typically include hundreds and thousands of repeating units. Show the class how flexible the chain is by leading it around the room, weaving between the desks and chairs. Have another group of 4–5 students stand in a line and form another polymer chain parallel to the first chain. Have the chains move around as before. Note that the movement of one chain does not depend on the movement of any other unless the chains get very close to each other. Add crosslinkers between the polymer chains by assigning students not already in the chains to hold onto both chains at once. The movement of one chain now is influenced by the movements of others; the crosslinkers hold the chains together. Show this by having the chains try to move in the same direction. The crosslinkers will need to move also. Now have the chains move in opposite directions. The crosslink bonds must break from one of the chains. If the chains are moved back together, the crosslinks can reform in new places or in the same places. This concept can also be shown by having two long chains of paper clips joined by a few "crosslinking" clips. (See Figure 13.)

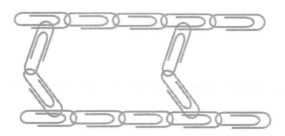

Figure 13: Dramatization of crosslinking a polymer

Individual and Group Projects

Several different projects can be assigned to the students, including the following:

- Collect and classify plastic samples using a classification system that they devise (e.g., according to their use, such as recreation, comfort and convenience, safety, economy, construction, communications, transportation). These classification systems can be compared with a classification system such as a resin code (letters and/or numbers inside a triangle shaped from three arrows) on the bottom of the plastic sample indicating the type of plastic.

- Write a library research report on a specific type of plastic including the properties of this plastic as well as the products and uses that can be derived from it. Students may even be asked to think of a new way to use the plastic or a new product that might be produced from it.

- Bring in newspaper and magazine articles about developments and/or uses of plastics. Organize these articles on bulletin boards or in notebooks.

- Write a report on polymer manufacturing techniques. Some of the most widely used techniques are blow molding, injection molding, casting, extrusion, and coating.

- List how plastics have changed or improved a given product over a previous version made from other materials (e.g., the advantages of a plastic bottle over a glass bottle).

- Research the role of catalysts in chemical reactions. Also research the mining, processing, cost, and use of a rare metal as a catalyst.

Cooperative Learning Strategies

Students can be divided into teams in order to manufacture a given polymer using varying materials. (For example: Glue Putty can be crosslinked by borax.) Each team can test their own product and compare it to their neighbors. By comparing results, the teams can pick their favorite product or recommend a given product for a specific purpose.

Cross-Curricular Strategies

Have students research the synthetic polymers used in clothing fibers and compare them to natural polymeric fibers. Consumer science teachers may be able to help here. Cotton, linen, silk, and wool are natural fibers. Synthetic fibers include nylon, acetate, acrylic, spandex (polyurethane), polypropylene, polyester, and rayon. List the properties and compare the uses of natural and synthetic fibers. Test fibers by placing them in acids and bases, heating them, stretching or tearing them, or by placing them in ultraviolet (window) light for long periods of time and watching for color and durability changes.

Biology and health classes might discuss the role of biochemical polymers (e.g. proteins and complex carbohydrates). Discuss biochemical catalysts (enzymes) that participate in living systems and industry.

Science-Technology-Society (S-T-S) Links

Technology. The module activities on polyethylene could serve as the basis for investigating a chemical compound. In developing a term project, have students trace the formation of the product from its starting materials, do a cost analysis, and address safety and handling concerns and regulatory compliance. Have students trace the polymer's path through various manufacturing processes that result in a wide variety of final products. This will help students gain an understanding of the role of chemistry in industry and how technology and society are affected by the science.

Classroom Company. Have students form their own "company" to produce and test their own plastic polymers. Slime and the white glue polymer are well suited for such a project. Students are given specific jobs, such as research and development, manufacturing, advertising, and finance, and must learn to work together to produce a given polymer product and sell it (or pretend to sell it) to other students. Students will need to determine how to obtain and organize needed materials to make a product, to compute the amounts of materials needed and their cost, to develop a need for their product (if sales are possible within the school), to compute their final profit or loss, and to determine how the profit or loss will be handled. Students learn that all persons must carry out their own jobs in order for a company to be successful. While involved in such activities, students will have to work as a team and use math, English, and creative skills for their company to be successful. Cooperative skills develop as the students become increasingly involved in their project.

Environmental Links. Explore the topics of recycling and waste disposal. Have students list properties that make a plastic reusable or properties that tend to create landfill and other waste disposal problems. This discussion could branch into a unit on environmental science.

Annotated List of Activities and Demonstrations

To aid you in choosing activities for your classroom, we have included an annotated list of activities and demonstrations. This listing includes information about the grade level that can benefit most from an activity and a brief description of each activity. A Curriculum Placement Guide follows this list.

1. **Identification of Plastics** (upper elementary to high school)
   Using seven common plastics, students carry out several tests including combustion and density to determine distinctive properties. Students then use this data to determine the identity of an unknown sample of plastic.

2. **The Rubber Band Stretch** (upper elementary to high school)
   Students determine what happens when a rubber band is stretched. (Heat is released.) They then discover the effects of heating a stretched rubber band.

3. **Needle through a Balloon** (elementary to high school)
   In this activity students learn the science behind the old magician trick to find that properties of the latex polymer make the trick possible.

4. **The Stretch Test** (upper elementary to high school)
   Students discover that some plastics (including Saran® wrap) stretch and break more easily in one direction than the other. The orientation of the polymer chains is established during the processing of the sheets.

5. **Water-Soluble Plastics** (high school)
   Students determine the solubility of polyvinyl alcohol as a function of temperature.

6. **Making a Polyester** (upper elementary to high school)
   In this activity, students react glycerol and phthalic anhydride to produce a hard, clear, thermoset polymer suitable for embedding objects like coins and marbles.

7. **Nylon 6-10** (high school)
   This activity demonstrates a condensation polymerization as sebacoyl chloride and hexamethylenediamine produce a thin rope of nylon 6-10. The product is formed through an interfacial process and pulled from the boundary of the two liquids.

8. **Making Polyvinyl Alcohol Fibers** (middle to high school)
   This activity demonstrates an alternative method to produce polyvinyl alcohol fibers from a reaction of polyvinyl alcohol solution and acetone. The demonstration uses the same interfacial process as the Nylon 6-10 activity.

9. **Comparison of Paper, Polyethylene, and Tyvek** (upper elementary to high school)
   The physical strength and water permeability of each of these polymer sheets are compared. The rate of evaporation of the water from each sample can be calculated.

10. **Producing Ethylene from Common Materials** (middle to high school)
    In this activity, polyethylene and paraffin oil are heated to produce ethylene gas. The ethylene is collected by displacement of water and checked for unsaturation (double bonds) using bromine water.

11. **Making Rubber Bands** (elementary to high school)
    Students make their own rubber bands from liquid latex, which is a crosslinked polymer. The crosslinking within the polymer is what causes the rubber band to reassume its original shape after stretching.

12. **Painting with Elastomers** (elementary to high school)
The students use tinted liquid latex to decorate personal items like T-shirts, scarves, or hats. The latex is stabilized with ammonia which can be neutralized using vinegar. Once the ammonia is removed, the latex hardens and becomes permanent.

13. **Making Erasers** (upper elementary to high school)
Students create erasers using liquid latex and items such as sand, salt, flour, and corn starch. After the erasers have cured, students test their erasers' properties.

14. **Glue Polymer** (elementary to high school)
Students choose from three different recipes to create a crosslinked polymer from white glue. They further test the putty by dehydrating and rehydrating the polymer, as well as testing it with vinegar and household ammonia.

15. **Homemade "Slimes"** (elementary to high school)
In this activity, the students add borax to polyvinyl alcohol, creating a crosslinked polymer similar to Slime® found in toy stores. The students conduct a Slime Olympics where they investigate the properties of this polymer by stretching it, compressing it, and bouncing it.

16. **Making a Super Ball** (middle to high school)
Students make silicone plastic balls from sodium silicate and ethyl alcohol and test the balls' bounce-ability.

17. **A Water-Absorbent Polymer** (upper elementary to high school)
Sodium polyacrylate will absorb about 800 times its own mass in distilled water. Students test the absorbent ability of this polymer for several other common liquids.

18. **Cellophane Tape Kaleidoscope** (elementary to high school)
In this activity, students construct a kaleidoscope from a cardboard tube, a paper cup, two pieces of Polaroid® sheet, and some cellophane tape. The layers of cellophane rotate the polarized light, causing different colors to appear.

19. **Friendly Plastic** (upper elementary to middle school)
Friendly Plastic® can be heated and formed into fun shapes. The wonderful advantage of this type of plastic is that if your first attempt is unsatisfactory, the plastic can be reheated and reshaped.

20. **Epoxy Putty** (elementary to middle school)
Unlike Friendly Plastic, epoxy putty is a type of polymer that permanently sets when it is heated (thermoset). Students can make fun shapes and designs but they must remember that once the putty has hardened, it cannot be reshaped.

21. **The Amazing Shrinking Plastic** (upper elementary to high school)
In this activity, students determine the amount of shrinkage of different plastics. They can also make earrings or pendants and shrink them.

22. **Taking the Foam Out of Styrofoam** (upper elementary to high school)
Students remove the gas from Styrofoam using acetone and observe as the polystyrene shrivels into a small, solid glob. They then examine the dried, de-foamed polystyrene.

23. **Molding Plastics** (middle to high school)
In this activity, students explore one type of plastic molding, extrusion blow molding, and make their own plastic bottles.

Topics

Activities	Nature of Matter	Science and Technology	Scientific Method	Health	Mass, Volume, and Density	Chemical Reactivity	Polymers	Oxidation-Reduction Reactions
1 Identification of Plastics	•	•	•		•	•	•	•
2 The Rubber Band Stretch	•	•	•		•		•	
3 Needle through a Balloon	•	•	•		•		•	
4 The Stretch Test	•	•	•		•		•	
5 Water-Soluble Plastics	•	•	•	•	•	•	•	
6 Making a Polyester	•	•	•		•	•	•	
7 Nylon 6-10	•	•	•		•	•	•	
8 Making Polyvinyl Alcohol Fibers	•	•	•			•	•	
9 Comparison of Paper, Polyethylene, and Tyvek	•	•	•				•	
10 Producing Ethylene from Common Materials	•	•	•		•	•	•	
11 Making Rubber Bands	•	•	•			•	•	
12 Painting with Elastomers	•	•	•			•	•	
13 Making Erasers	•	•	•		•	•	•	
14 Glue Polymer	•	•				•	•	

Topics

Activities	Nature of Matter	Science and Technology	Scientific Method	Health	Mass, Volume, and Density	Chemical Reactivity	Polymers	Oxidation-Reduction Reactions
15 Homemade "Slimes"	•							
16 Making a Super Ball	•	•	•		•	•	•	
17 A Water-Absorbent Polymer	•	•	•	•	•	•	•	
18 Cellophane Tape Kaleidoscope	•	•	•		•	•	•	
19 Friendly Plastic	•	•	•		•		•	
20 Epoxy Putty	•	•	•			•	•	
21 The Amazing Shrinking Plastic	•	•	•		•		•	
22 Taking the Foam Out of Styrofoam	•	•	•		•	•	•	
23 Molding Plastics	•	•	•		•		•	

Activities and Demonstrations

Identification of Plastics

Students are provided with information to identify seven common polymers using various tests, including density and combustion. An unknown plastic from a commercial product can then be identified using the density and combustion data.

Recommended Grade Level .... **9–12 as a hands-on activity**
4–8 as a demonstration
Group Size .... **1–4 students**
Time for Preparation .... **30–35 minutes**
Time for Procedure .... **45–55 minutes**

Materials

Opening Strategy
- large samples of the 7 polymers listed for the Procedure
- large sample of 1 of the 7 polymers to use as an unknown

Procedure
Per Group
- 1 of the following sources of heat:
  - long fireplace matches
  - a burning candle
- samples of the following 7 polymers:
  - cellulose acetate (CA)—overhead projector sheets, Ping-Pong™ balls
  - polypropylene (PP)—yogurt containers (recycle code 5)
  - low-density polyethylene (LDPE)—dry cleaning bags (recycle code 4)
  - high-density polyethylene (HDPE)—milk jugs (recycle code 2)
  - polyethylene terephthalate (PETE)—2-L bottles (recycle code 1)
  - polyvinyl chloride (PVC)—dish detergent bottles (recycle code 3)
  - polystyrene (PS)—clear plastic cups (recycle code 6)

 Do not use foamed polystyrene.

- samples of polymers for unknowns:
  - any samples listed above
- 15-cm (6-in) length of 18-gauge copper wire
- stirring rod or spoon
- scissors for cutting polymer samples
- cork
- tongs, forceps, or tweezers
- goggles

Per Class
- 180 mL rubbing alcohol (70% isopropyl alcohol solution)
- 80 mL (⅓ cup) table sugar (sucrose)
- 4 small, wide-mouthed jars with lids
- permanent marker and labels
- 100-mL graduated cylinder
- pliers
- bowls (for rinsing plastic samples)
- paper towels
- (optional) 1 drop Lysol® Deodorizing Cleaner

Variation
- samples of the 7 polymers
- 1 M hydrochloric acid solution (HCl)
- 1 M sodium hydroxide solution (NaOH)
- rubbing alcohol
- vegetable oil
- about 500 mL 91–99% isopropyl alcohol solution or 95–98% ethyl alcohol solution
- 1-L graduated cylinder or 1-L bottle with the top cut off
- samples of low-density and high-density polyethylene

Resources

Hydrochloric acid, sodium hydroxide and ethyl alcohol can be purchased from a chemical supply company such as Flinn Scientific, P.O. Box 219, Batavia, IL 60510-0219, 800/452-1261.

- 1 M hydrochloric acid—catalog #H0013 for 500 mL
- 1 M sodium hydroxide—catalog #S0148 for 500 mL
- 95% ethyl alcohol—catalog #E0009 for 500 mL

All samples of polymers, 70% and 91–99% isopropyl alcohol solutions, vegetable oil, and table sugar can be purchased from a grocery store or pharmacy. Copper wire can be purchased at a hardware store.

Safety and Disposal

Goggles should be worn while preparing for and when performing this activity.

The laboratory should be well ventilated using a fan or by means of a fume hood. Burning plastic, especially polyvinyl chloride, can create unpleasant and/or toxic fumes. To minimize the problem, use small pieces of plastic (1-cm x 2.5-cm). Polyvinyl chloride is particularly problematic in that it gives off hydrochloric acid fumes; be sure to keep the sample size small to minimize fumes. Proper fire safety should be exercised. This includes working on a flame-resistant surface and removing unnecessary flammable materials from the area. Long-haired people should tie hair back when working near a flame.

The dilute solutions of hydrochloric acid (HCl) or sodium hydroxide (NaOH) used in the Variation can cause serious chemical burns. Handle these solutions with care to avoid skin and eye contact. Should contact occur, rinse the affected area. If the contact involves the eyes, medical attention should be sought while the rinsing is occurring.

The wire may have sharp ends; take appropriate precautions.

Rubbing alcohol is intended for external use only. Excess quantities of the solutions used in this experiment can be safely and legally disposed of by flushing down the sink or stored for future use.

Getting Ready

The unknown polymer sample should be cut into pieces about 1 cm x 2.5 cm and labeled to identify the type of product it came from ahead of time.

Cut the seven known polymers into 1-cm x 2.5-cm strips and label them ahead of time using the polymer recycle code or common abbreviations given in Materials.

Prepare the copper wire for each group by bending a small loop on the end of each piece of wire using a pair of pliers. Insert the straight end of the copper wire into one end of the cork. The cork functions as a handle for holding the copper wire during the flame test.

Prepare the solutions of known density as shown in Table 1. Put all of the solutions into small, wide-mouthed jars with lids so the liquids will not evaporate. (If sugar solution is to be saved for future use, add a drop of Lysol Deodorizing Cleaner to prevent bacterial growth.)

Table 1: Solutions of Known Density

Solution	Components	Density
A	100 mL 70% isopropyl alcohol solution/40 mL water	0.91 g/mL
B	80 mL 70% isopropyl alcohol solution/40 mL water	0.93 g/mL
C	150 mL water	1.00 g/mL
D	80 mL (⅓ cup) sugar/150 mL water	1.14 g/mL

If students perform the activity as a group, give each group a different type of plastic. Set up four work stations, each with a different solution from Table 1, a few paper towels, and a pair of tongs, forceps, or tweezers. At the station with the sugar solution, be sure to set out a labeled bowl or pan of water for rinsing the plastic samples.

Have the students prepare a data chart to record their observations.

Opening Strategy

Have large samples of the eight polymers to be tested (seven known, one unknown) at the front of the classroom. Ask students if they know what kinds of plastic are used in the different items. Discuss recycle codes and their meanings. Ask students how they could tell the difference between the different kinds of plastics. (The students should indicate that some kind of test should be performed.)

Procedure

Part 1: Relative Density

Try both of the following methods and decide which works best for determining the relative density of each of the known and unknown samples in Solution A. Compare results with those obtained by other students to determine a density range for each of the known plastic samples.

Method A

1. Drop one of the known samples into Solution A. Record whether it floats or sinks. (Be certain that the sample breaks the surface tension of the solution to prevent any false observations.)

2. Remove the sample with the forceps, rinse with water, and dry it off.

3. Repeat Steps 1–2 until the other six known polymer samples and the unknown have been tested in Solution A.

Method B

1. Place all of the known polymer samples together into Solution A and stir. Note which samples sink and float.

2. Remove the samples with the forceps, rinse with water, and dry them.

Part 2: A Flame Test

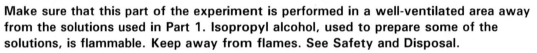

Make sure that this part of the experiment is performed in a well-ventilated area away from the solutions used in Part 1. Isopropyl alcohol, used to prepare some of the solutions, is flammable. Keep away from flames. See Safety and Disposal.

1. Set up the heat source and begin to heat a clean, dry sample of one of the seven known polymers except the PVC, using tongs to hold the sample in the edge of the flame. Observe and record the results of testing the ease with which the sample ignites, the color of the flame, the color of the smoke, the odor, and the aftereffect of removing the sample from the flame. Repeat this procedure until the six known (non-PVC) polymers have been tested. Compare the results with those in Table 2.

2. For the polyvinyl chloride (PVC) sample only: Place the small loop at the end of the piece of copper wire into the flame for 30 seconds or until it is red hot. Take the wire out of the flame and place the sample of PVC on the hot loop. Place the loop and PVC sample back into the flame. It should burn with a green flame.

3. Repeat Step 1 for the unknown polymer sample. Only repeat Step 2 if you expect the unknown to be PVC.

Part 3: Interpreting the Data

Compare the results of both the flame tests and the density tests for the unknown polymer sample with the data for the seven known samples. From this comparison, decide on the identity of the unknown sample.

Table 2: Combustion Tests of Polymers

Polymer	Abbreviation and Recycle Code	Repeating Monomer Unit	Observations with Heating
polyethylene and polypropylene (Polyethylene melts faster than polypropylene.)	LDPE—#4 HDPE—#2 PP—#5	$-CH_2-CH_2-$ (polyethylene) $-CH_2-CH-$ (polypropylene) $\quad\quad\quad\ \ \vert$ $\quad\quad\quad CH_3$	Ignites: easily Flame: yellow with blue base Smoke: little (white) Smell: paraffin wax (drips like a burning candle) Removal from flame: burns
polyvinyl chloride	PVC—#3	$-CH_2-CH-$ $\quad\quad\quad\ \vert$ $\quad\quad\quad Cl$	Ignites: with difficulty Flame: yellow with green base Smoke: white Smell: very acrid (strong acid) Removal from flame: does not burn In flame: burns with a green flame on a hot copper wire
polystyrene	PS—#6	$-CH_2-CH-$ (with benzene ring)	Ignites: easily Flame: deep yellow Smoke: sooty black Smell: like "smelly" plastic Removal from flame: burns, does not drip, leaves little ash
cellulose acetate	CA	(cellulose acetate structure)	Ignites: easily Flame: pale yellow Smoke: white Smell: vinegar Removal from flame: burns
polyethylene terephthalate	PETE—#1	$-O-(CH_2)_2-O-C-$ (benzene ring) $-C-$ with $=O$ groups	Ignites: easily Flame: deep yellow Smoke: sooty black Smell: slight Removal from flame: burns a short time, then drips, leaves little ash

Variation

- Perform a demonstration to distinguish between low-density polyethylene (LDPE) and high-density polyethylene (HDPE). Cut the LDPE sample in the shape of an "L" and the HDPE sample in the shape of an "H." Make the width of the letters almost the same as the diameter of a 1-L graduated cylinder or 1-L bottle so they will float in an upright position where they can easily be seen by the class. Fill a 1-L, transparent graduated cylinder or a 1-L bottle with the top cut off with an alcohol/water solution made by mixing equal amounts of water and either 95–98% ethyl alcohol solution or 91–99% isopropyl alcohol solution. Drop samples of LDPE and HDPE into the cylinder. The HDPE sample should sink to the bottom while the LDPE sample should float near the top.

Discussion

- Discuss the results of the density and flame tests for each known polymer sample. Ask students to explain how this information can be used to determine the identity of the unknown. Did they need the results of both tests?
  The results of both tests provide important clues to the identity of the unknown; neither test alone provides sufficiently unique results to rule out all other plastic samples (unless the unknown is one of the few that provided a uniquely colored flame).

- Ask students to speculate how recyclers might use the relative density test in separating plastics.
  Each plastic has a specific density range. Recyclers shred the plastic samples and place them in solutions of different known densities. Any polymer pieces that float in a given solution are removed from the solution. The remaining pieces are placed into a slightly denser solution, and this process is repeated with solutions of increasing density until all of the plastics have been separated.

- Ask students to suggest reasons for wanting to separate different plastics in waste.
  Since plastics can be melted and reshaped, it makes sense to reuse the plastics rather than placing them in a landfill. Recycling codes make identifying different types of plastic easier.

Explanation

A material that is more dense than a given liquid will sink in that liquid, while a material that is less dense will float. For example, corks and oil will float in water because they are less dense than water; pennies and syrup will sink in water because they are more dense than water.

It is possible to estimate the density (mass/volume) of a material by observing its sinking or floating behavior in solutions of known density. In this activity, the approximate densities of various polymers are determined by making such observations. For example, if high-density polyethylene (HDPE) sinks in Solution B (density 0.93 g/mL) but floats in Solution C (density 1.00 g/mL), then its density must be greater than that of Solution B, but less than that of Solution C. Therefore, the density of HDPE must lie between 0.93 and 1.00 g/mL. Table 3 lists the typical ranges of densities for the polymers used in this activity, as well as their sinking or floating behavior in Solutions A, B, C, and D.

This relative density (floating/sinking) technique has practical applications in identification of materials and in recycling efforts. By dumping shredded plastics into a very low-density solution, removing the shreds that float, dumping the remaining shreds into a slightly denser solution, again removing the shreds that float, and continuing this process using denser solutions, it is possible to separate the plastics by their densities and thus their type.

Table 3: Typical Ranges of Densities for Seven Polymers

Polymer	Density Range (in g/mL)	Solutions (density in g/mL)*			
		A (0.91)	B (0.93)	C (1.00)	D (1.14)
cellulose acetate (CA)	1.3	sink	sink	sink	sink
polypropylene (PP)	0.90–0.91	float	float	float	float
low-density polyethylene (LDPE)	0.92–0.94	sink	***	float	float
high-density polyethylene (HDPE)	0.95–0.97	sink	sink	float	float
polystyrene (PS)**	1.05–1.07	sink	sink	sink	float
polyethylene terephthalate (PETE)	1.38–1.39	sink	sink	sink	sink
polyvinyl chloride (PVC)	1.16–1.35	sink	sink	sink	sink

*	As prepared in Table 1
**	Do not use foamed polystyrene
***	Depends upon the sample tested

It is often possible to identify an unknown by observing and comparing its properties to that of a series of knows. Density alone, however, will not distinguish all of the polymers from each other. In this activity, flammability was also determined. Polymers within given classifications often burn with characteristic flames. Cellulose acetate (CA, polyvinyl acetate), for example, is very flammable, burning quickly with a characteristic vinegar odor. This vinegar smell is due to the liberation of the acetate group upon heating of the polymer. Vinegar is about 5% acetic acid. On the other hand, when molded on a copper wire, polyvinyl chloride (PVC) burns with a yellow-green flame. This color is due to the reaction of the copper wire and the chlorine from the polymer. Polymers such as polystyrene (PS) and polyethylene terephthalate (PETE) burn with a smoky flame because of their structures. Both compounds contain a benzene ring as part of their structure, and the unsaturation is responsible for the smoky flame when either polymer is burned.

Together relative density and flammability are useful in characterizing polymers. While tests described in this activity cannot positively identify all unknown plastics, they can help distinguish between many common ones. Limitations occur because some plastics can be so similar in density that they are indistinguishable by the known density solutions used in the activity. Others may not only be so dense as to sink in the most dense solution, but also may be indistinguishable by the flame test described in Part 2.

Key Science Concepts

- density
- flame test
- polymers and their properties

Cross-Curricular Integration

Art
Have students make sculptures or collages using various plastics.

Language Arts
Have the students speculate as to developments and uses of plastics in the future and write stories describing these new uses.

References

The Dow Chemical Company. *Identifying Rigid Plastic Containers,* Form Number 304-189-989X.

"Identifying Polymers by Density and a Flame Test;" *Fun With Chemistry: A Guidebook of K–12 Activities;* Sarquis, M., Sarquis, J., Eds.; Institute of Chemical Education: Madison, WI, 1993; Vol. 2, pp 107–112.

Kolb, K.E., Kolb, D.K. "A Quick, Simple Demonstration to Distinguish Between HD and LD Polyethylene," *Journal of Chemical Education.* 1986, 63, 417.

Salters Chemistry Course. "Plastics," Science Education Group: Heslington, York, Great Britain.

Sherman, M. "Polymers Link Science and Fun," presentation at a workshop funded in part by the Industrial Sponsors, American Chemical Society, Polymer Chemistry Division, Washington, D.C., August 1993.

The Rubber Band Stretch

What happens when a polymer like rubber is heated? The answer may surprise you.

Recommended Grade Level 4–12
Group Size .... demonstration or groups of 1–4 students
Time for Preparation .... 5 minutes
Time for Procedure .... 30–45 minutes

Materials

Opening Strategy
- ring stand
- small ring clamp
- glass bottle or beaker with diameter slightly larger than that of the ring clamp
- Bunsen burner

Procedure, Part 1
Per Class
- ring stand
- utility clamp
- heat gun (A hair dryer can be substituted, but the effect is less dramatic.)
- object with a mass of 100 g to 1 kg (Weights from a balance work well.)
- rubber band about 150 mm long x 5 mm wide (about 6 in x ¼ in)
- (optional) meterstick

Procedure, Part 2
Per Class
- long rope

Procedure, Part 3
Per Student
- small rubber bands (1 per student)

Variation
- plastic grocery bags and/or dry cleaning bags
- (optional) plastic holders from beverage six-packs

Safety and Disposal

Exercise caution when handling the ring clamp in Introducing the Activity—it will remain hot for some time after heating. Allow the ring to cool to room temperature before removing it from the ring stand.

Getting Ready

1. Cut the large rubber band to make a strip, and hang the strip from a clamp on a ring stand.

2. The minimum amount of mass required to provide an easily measurable difference in the length of the rubber band will depend on the width of the rubber band. Use the combinations in Table 1 as a guide.

Table 1: Rubber Band-Mass Combinations

Width of Rubber Band	Recommended Mass
3.5 mm or less	100 g
3.5 mm to 6.0 mm	500 g
6.0 mm to 10.0 mm	1 kg

Opening Strategy

Show students how metals react when they are heated: Set up a ring stand with a small ring clamp attached to it. Demonstrate that a glass bottle or beaker will not pass through the ring. (Make sure that the diameter of the bottle or beaker is just barely larger than the ring diameter so that when the ring is heated, the bottle will drop through.)

Heat the ring with a Bunsen burner. Pass the bottle or beaker through the ring and catch it to prevent it from breaking. Ask the students what allowed the bottle to pass through the ring. (The metal ring expanded when it was heated, making the diameter of the ring larger. Since the diameter of the ring increased, the bottle was able to pass through the ring.) Ask the students to predict what the rubber band will do when it is heated.

Procedure

Part 1: The Challenge

1. Tie a rubber band to a ring clamp attached to a ring stand. Hang a weight from the rubber band so that the weight just barely touches the base of the ring stand or the top of the table.

2. Encourage the students to predict what will happen when the rubber band is heated.

3. Heat the entire rubber band with the heat gun, moving the gun up and down the length of the rubber band, as shown in Figure 1.

 If the rubber band is heated too much in one spot, it may melt and/or break.

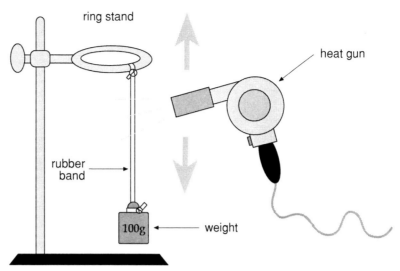

Figure 1: Heating the rubber band with a heat gun

4. Observe the position of the weight. When the rubber band contracts, the weight rises from the ring stand or bench top.

5. (optional) Use a meterstick to measure the amount the rubber band contracts. Measure the height of the weight from the table top and then remeasure the height after heating.

Part 2: The Kinesthetic Enactment

1. Have several students hold on to a long rope at regular intervals and stretch it across the room as shown in Figure 2. Define the rope as being part of a polymer chain in the rubber band, and note that the polymer chain is stretched to its limit.

Figure 2: Stretched polymer chain

2. Warming the rubber band gives energy to the atoms in the chain which in turn causes increased molecular motion. To simulate this increased molecular motion, the students in the middle of the rope should move back and forth, perpendicular to the length of the rope. The students at the ends will need to move inwards appropriately. This movement can occur only if the distance between the two ends decreases. (See Figure 3.) This is analogous to the rubber band becoming shorter as it is heated.

Figure 3: The polymer chain being heated

3. For the rubber band to stretch again, it must lose the energy it gained in Step 2. This loss of energy decreases the molecular motion, and the ends move farther apart. To simulate the loss of energy and the lengthening of the rubber band, have students return to their original positions.

Part 3: The Hot Upper Lip

1. Touch a rubber band to the skin above your upper lip or forehead and determine if it feels hot or cold to your skin. Record this observation.

2. Predict what will happen to the temperature when the rubber band stretches. Stretch the rubber band and quickly touch it to your upper lip or forehead again. Describe the temperature as warmer or cooler to your skin than the unstretched rubber band. Record the observation.

3. Predict what will happen to the temperature when the rubber band contracts. Stretch the rubber band and press the stretched rubber band against your lip or forehead. Then allow the rubber band to contract rapidly while still holding it against your upper lip or forehead. Describe the temperature of the contracted rubber band as warmer or cooler to your skin than the stretched rubber band. Record this observation.

Variation

- The students could also test other polymers in Parts 1 and 3 to see if they behave in the same way as the rubber band. Examples of different polymers that could be tested would be the plastic holder for a six-pack of soda pop or fruit juice, a plastic grocery bag, or a dry-cleaning bag. When these plastics are stretched, they distort, becoming thinner and thinner in one spot. This process is called "necking down." It will produce even more heat than the stretching of a rubber band. (See Figure 4.)

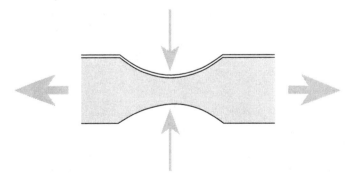

Figure 4: Necking down a plastic strip

Discussion

- Ask students to explain why the rubber band shrank in length when heated. *See the Explanation.*

- Have students relate how the observations for the rubber band stretch in Part 1 and The Hot Upper Lip in Part 3 were explained by the Kinesthetic Enactment in Part 2. *To stretch a rubber band, the rubber band must lose excess energy. In Part 3, this energy is transferred to your lip, accounting for the warmth that was felt. For a rubber band to contract, it must gain energy. In Part 1, the heat from the heat gun supplied the energy and in Part 3, the heat from your upper lip supplied the energy. That is why the contracted rubber band feels cooler than the stretched rubber band.*

Explanation

Many materials expand during heating, but many polymers, such as rubber bands, contract when heated because of the increased molecular motion. This effect is demonstrated in Part 2 of the activity, where the students represent the individual molecules and the rope represents the strong bonds between the molecules in the polymer chain. When a rubber band is pulled taut, the movements of the molecules are restricted by their bonding. However, the energy that they possessed while moving randomly does not disappear. (A process that liberates heat, such as stretching a rubber band, is known as an exothermic process. One that absorbs heat—heating the rubber band to make it contract—is an endothermic process.) The process occurring in Part 3 is summarized in Figure 5.

stretched rubber band + heat ⇌ contracted rubber band

Figure 5: Heating the rubber band makes it contract.

The direction that the process will take can be predicted from LeChatelier's principle; adding heat to the system shifts the process toward the contracted form, while cooling the system causes a shift toward the stretched state.

For an explanation on the basis of the entropy changes see the Chang reference.

Key Science Concepts

- endothermic/exothermic changes
- equilibrium/LeChatelier's principle
- polymers and their properties

Cross-Curricular Integration

Language Arts
Have students develop advertisements for polymers that shrink when you heat them.

Mathematics
Have students calculate the ratio of the length of the rubber band before and after heating. They could also calculate the percent of change in the length of the rubber band.

References

Chang, R. *Chemistry*, 3rd ed.; Random House: New York, 1988; p 990.

"Rubber Band Stretch;" *Fun With Chemistry: A Guidebook of K–12 Activities;* Sarquis, M., Sarquis, J., Eds.; Institute for Chemical Education: Madison, WI, 1991; Vol. 1, pp 167–172.

Needle through a Balloon

How does a magician push a needle through a balloon without popping it? Is it just "magic" or can science help us to explain this trick? In this activity students discover that an understanding of some of the unique characteristics of polymers can help us to perform a trick that seems to defy common sense.

Recommended Grade Level 2–12
Group Size .... 1–4 students
Time for Preparation .... none
Time for Procedure .... 5 minutes

Materials

Procedure
Per Group
- latex balloons (not longer than pointed object chosen below)
- 1 of the following pointed objects:
  - bamboo skewer
  - 30–35 cm (12–14 in) upholstery needle
  - sharpened knitting needle
  - coat hanger wire sharpened to a point
- 1 of the following lubricants (enough to half-fill a cap from a 2-L bottle):
  - cooking oil
  - petroleum jelly
  - dishwashing liquid
- (optional) paper towel or cloth
- goggles

Variation
Per Class
- upholstery needle
- yarn or string

Extensions
Per Group
- penny
- zipper-type plastic bag
- sharpened pencil
- tub or basin

Resources

Latex balloons can be purchased from a magic store, floral shop, department store, or a balloon store. If large quantities are required, balloons may be purchased from National Latex Products, 246 E. 4th St., Ashland, OH 44805, 419/289-3300. There is a minimum order for mail orders.

Upholsterer's needles may be available from an upholstery shop, mattress factory, or a sewing supply store. You may also want to check magic and theatrical supply stores for the long needles used in the balloon-piercing trick. Bamboo skewers can be purchased from a grocery store.

Safety and Disposal

Goggles should be worn when performing this activity. For personal safety, store the needle with the point inserted in a cork when not in use. (This also keeps the needle point from becoming dull.) The opening strategy suggests inserting bamboo skewers into the balloon until it pops or deflates. Be sure to use only bamboo skewers for this demonstration so that metal needles or sharpened coat hangers will not become projectiles when the balloon breaks.

Opening Strategy

Act as if you are a magician and awe your audience with your magical powers by inserting a bamboo skewer into a balloon without popping it. Challenge the students to predict how many skewers you can place in the balloon before it pops or deflates. Then continue to insert bamboo skewers into the balloon until it pops or deflates.

Procedure

1. Inflate the balloon and tie the opening. (Have the balloon slightly underinflated, so that it will be easier to puncture without breaking. Make sure the balloon is not longer than the needle or skewer.)

2. Dip the tip of the bamboo skewer or needle into a small container of lubricant and use a paper towel, cloth, or your fingers to spread the oil along the entire length of the needle or skewer.

3. Insert the skewer or needle with a gentle twisting motion into the nipple end of the balloon (the end opposite the knot). The rubber is thickest here. (See Figure 1.)

Figure 1: Twist the skewer into the nipple end of the balloon.

4. Continue pushing and twisting the needle or skewer until the tip emerges from the other side close to the tied end. The balloon will not burst. (See Figure 2.)

Figure 2: The needle emerges from the end of the balloon.

5. Push the needle or skewer all the way through the balloon so that it comes out at the tied end.

6. Place your hand over the holes to feel the air leaking out.

7. To show that this was a real balloon, jab the needle through the side where the rubber is stretched. The balloon will pop!

Variation

- Use an upholstery needle that has an eye. Thread yarn or string through the eye. See how many balloons you can string together.

Extensions

- Place a penny inside the balloon before inflating it. Puncture the balloon at the nipple end with a needle or skewer. Remove the needle or skewer and turn the balloon so that the penny covers the hole inside the balloon. Turn the balloon so that the hole and the penny are on top. The air pressure inside the balloon will hold the penny in place. Move the balloon around. The penny will stay secured over the hole.

- Fill a zipper-type plastic bag with water and poke a sharpened pencil all the way through so that it protrudes from both sides. Ask the students to apply what they have learned from the balloon activity to explain why the water does not leak out around the pencil. Do this activity over a tub or basin just in case the seal on the plastic bag opens or the pencil is pulled out of the bag.

Discussion

- Discuss what happens to the balloon when the skewer is inserted near the nipple versus when the skewer is inserted on the side.
  The balloon does not burst when the skewer is inserted near the nipple of the balloon, but does burst when punctured on the side.

- Ask the students to explain the role the lubricant plays.
  When the lubricant is applied to the skewer, it helps the skewer to slide through the rubber more easily, minimizing the chance of a tear. Also, it partly seals the hole, minimizing air flow.

Explanation

Balloons are made commercially through a process called dip coating. A mold, called a mandrel, is lowered into a vat of liquid latex (natural rubber) then pulled out again so that a thin film of material is left adhering to it. The thin sheet of rubber that is formed contains many long intertwined polymer chains. The elasticity of these polymer chains causes rubber to be stretchy. Blowing up the balloon stretches these polymer chains. The strands in the middle region of the balloon stretch more than the regions at the tie and at the nipple end (opposite the tie), which are thicker due to the molding process. (See Figure 3.)

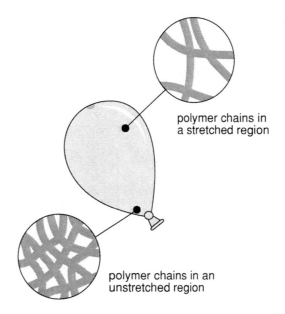

polymer chains in a stretched region

polymer chains in an unstretched region

Figure 3: Enlarged regions of balloon

When a sharp, lubricated needle pierces the thick ends of the rubber balloon, the polymer strands that make up the rubber are gently pushed aside. When the needle is removed, the air can be felt leaking out through the holes where the strands were pushed apart. The balloon will slowly deflate, not burst suddenly. In the second extension, the pencil used to puncture the zipper-type plastic bag of water serves the same purpose as the needle. The pencil pushed the strands of the polymer (polyethylene) apart without allowing the water to leak out. It is necessary to use a smooth, sharp needle, skewer, or pencil for this activity. A dull needle is more likely to tear the polymer chains.

When the balloon is given a quick jab to its side with the needle, it pops. The rubber is thin and the polymer chains are tightly stretched at the sides of the balloon. The polymer strands in this stretched region are unable to slide apart any further without tearing. Once a tear begins, it rapidly continues as the air rushes out, causing the balloon to pop.

Extra-thick-walled, latex balloons are available at magic shops. These special balloons allow you to push a needle through the sides as well as the ends.

Key Science Concepts

- gas pressure
- polymers and their properties

Cross-Curricular Integration

Art
Have the students construct various figures (such as animals) using balloons.

Language Arts
For younger students, read the book about balloons titled *The Red Balloon,* by Albert Lamorisse (Doubleday, ISBN 0-385-14297-8). In this story, a young boy finds a red balloon with a mind of its own floating across the skies of Paris.

Mathematics
Have the students determine the circumference of a cross-section of the balloon before and after the needle is pushed through it.

References

"Needle Through a Balloon;" *Fun With Chemistry: A Guidebook of K–12 Activities;* Sarquis, M., Sarquis, J., Eds.; Institute for Chemical Education: Madison, WI, 1991; Vol. 1, pp 139–142.

Toepker, T., Department of Physics, Xavier University, Cincinnati, OH, personal communication.

The Stretch Test

What happens when you try to stretch a thin piece of plastic? This activity provides an answer to this question as well as some interesting evidence about the way the plastic is made.

Recommended Grade Level 4–12
Group Size .... demonstration or groups of 1–4 students
Time for Preparation .... 20–30 minutes
Time for Procedure .... 20–30 minutes if demonstration
                                                           80–90 minutes if activity

Materials

Opening Strategy
- plastic grocery bag

Procedure
Per Group
- different brands of plastic wrap (e.g., Saran Wrap™, Glad® wrap, sandwich bag)
- ring stand
- ring clamp
- 12-in shoestring or cord
- 1 or 2 plastic 2-L bottles
- (optional) 1-kg weight
- permanent marker
- plastic tub to catch water
- scissors
- 100-mL graduated cylinder or 200-mL beaker
- plastic funnel

Variations
- lead weights or other heavy objects
- various brands of plastic garbage bags and grocery bags

Extension
- Teflon® tape (PTFE thread-seal tape)

Resources

The Teflon tape used in the extension can be purchased in the plumbing sections of hardware and discount department stores.

Getting Ready

Prepare widthwise strips of plastic wrap by carefully cutting three strips of plastic 5 cm x 30 cm (2 in x 12 in) parallel to the width. (See Figure 1.) Avoid introducing slight tears in the strips. Using a permanent marker, label these pieces "W" for width of the plastic wrap.

Prepare lengthwise strips of plastic wrap by carefully cutting three strips of plastic 5 cm x 30 cm (2 in x 12 in) parallel to the length of the roll of plastic wrap. (See Figure 1.) Avoid introducing tears in the strips. Using a permanent marker, label these pieces "L" for length of the plastic wrap.

 Carefully note the definitions of length and width shown in Figure 1.

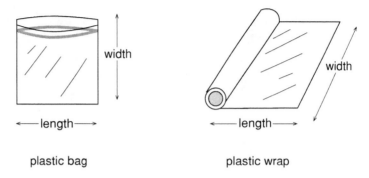

plastic bag   plastic wrap

Figure 1: Directions for cutting plastic wrap and plastic bags

Tie a shoestring or cord around the neck of a 2-L plastic bottle. Set up the ring stand and ring clamp as shown in Figure 2. (The polymer sample may stretch several inches—be sure to allow room for this. Placing the apparatus at the edge of a table with a plastic tub below it on the floor works well.)

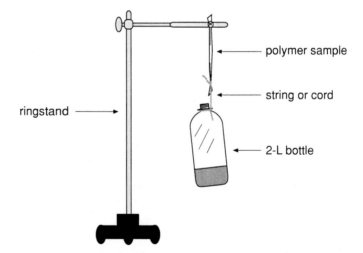

Figure 2: The apparatus for testing the plastic strips

Opening Strategy

The nature of polymer chains within a thin film can be shown through this simple kinesthetic activity. Have 4–5 students stand in a line facing the class. Define each student as being a monomer. Have the monomers link arms or hold hands. Each link represents a chemical bond. The chain they form has many units in it, simulating a polymer chain. Emphasize that polymers typically include hundreds and thousands of repeating units.

Have 1 or 2 more groups of 4–5 students stand in a line forming additional polymer chains parallel to the first chain as shown in Figure 3. Explain that plastic wrap can be made by pouring the polymer onto a conveyor belt and machining it into a thin film. When the films are made, the separate polymer chains will be pulled close together and aligned parallel to each other. (The chains are aligned in the machine direction.) Point out that while there may be some interactions between the two chains, these attractions are, however, much weaker than the linked arms which represent covalent bonds. Have one person hold the hands of the right ends of the polymer chains and have a second person hold the hands of the hands of the left ends of the chains. Have these two people pull the chains in opposite directions with equal force as shown by the large arrows in Figure 3a. Note that there is little or no net movement of the chains. Show this concept by stretching a handle of a plastic grocery bag. It will stretch but not break. Repeat this stretch test, but this time have two students pull the middles of the two outside chains apart as shown in Figure 3b. Note the ease of movement of the chains due to the lack of chemical bonds. Illustrate this concept by stretching the plastic grocery bag widthwise to show how easily it stretches and breaks.

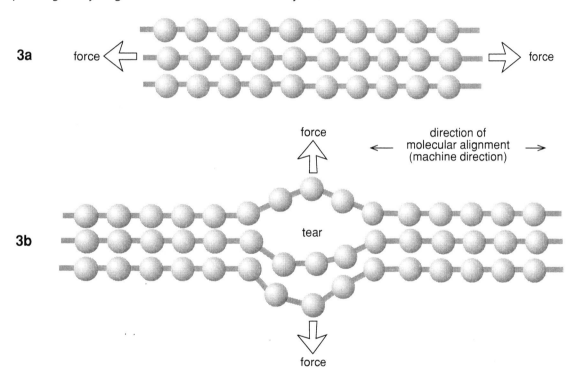

Figure 3: (a) Results of a force applied along polymer chains; (b) Results of a force applied across polymer chains

Procedure

1. Tie one end of a widthwise strip to the ring clamp and the opposite end to the shoestring tied to one of the 2-L bottles. (See Figure 2.) Avoid stretching the wrap. **It is very important that the plastic strips are not stretched before the weights are added. If the plastic is stretched, you will get false results.**

2. Slowly add water to the bottle using a funnel and a 100-mL graduated cylinder or 200-mL beaker. Keep track of how much water is added. Record the amount of water that finally causes the plastic strip to break. (Typically 0.5 L to 1 L is required.)

3. Repeat Steps 1 and 2 using the remaining widthwise strips. Record the amounts of water that caused the strips to break. Calculate the average volumes of water required to break the widthwise strips. Since the density of water is about 1.0 g/mL at room temperature, this volume (in mL) corresponds to the mass of water in grams.

4. Repeat Steps 1–3 with each of the lengthwise strips (L).
The lengthwise strips may require more than 2 L water. Add additional weight by placing a 1-kg weight in the bottom of the 2-L bottle or by placing an additional 2-L bottle on the shoestring or cord.

5. Repeat Steps 1–4 using another brand of plastic wrap or plastic sandwich bags.

Variations

- Instead of using the 2-L bottle and water, use lead weights or other heavy objects to test the strength of the plastic.

- Conduct the test to determine both the relative strength and orientation of the polymer strands for various brands of plastic garbage bags and grocery bags.

Extension

- Experiment with stretching plumber's Teflon tape (also known as PTFE thread-seal tape). This material can stretch to a remarkable degree along its width, while showing little or no stretch along its length. Furthermore, once the tape has been stretched widthwise it can be returned to its original shape. Have the students try writing their names or messages on a piece of tape. Have them stretch the tape until the words are completely distorted and unreadable, then have them stretch the tape back to its original shape—the message will once again be legible. The tape can be used to send secret messages.

Discussion

- Ask the students which orientation of the plastic held the most weight before breaking. *The lengthwise strips held the most weight before breaking.*

- Discuss why the lengthwise strip was stronger than the widthwise strip. *When the plastic film is made, the liquid polymer is stretched so that the polymer chains line up in the direction of the stretch. This becomes the length direction (machine direction) of the plastic. There are strong covalent bonds between the atoms in the polymer chains along the length of the plastic film, but there are only weak van der Waals forces between the chains along the width of the plastic film.*

Explanation

In this activity, the widthwise and lengthwise plastic strips stretched under the weight of the water and eventually broke but the lengthwise plastic strips required a much greater amount of water to cause them to break. These results are directly related to the manufacturing process used to make the plastic wrap.

During the manufacturing of plastic wrap, the plastic is rolled so that the long polymer chains align themselves roughly parallel to each other. In most plastic wraps (such as Saran, which is made from polyvinylidene chloride), the individual polymer chains are attracted only weakly to each other by what are termed van der Waals forces. These weak forces are easily overcome by an external force such as applied in this activity. Thus the plastic stretches and eventually breaks. (Refer to Figure 3.)

When the plastic is stretched lengthwise in the other direction, however, only little stretch is noted. This is because the chemical bonds are very strong. Plastics are made of hundreds of thousands of repeating units that are bonded together via covalent bonds between the adjacent carbon atoms within the polymer chains. The strength of these covalent bonds make these long, giant molecules especially strong. Thus only a slight give is observed when the polymer is stretched along the axis of these molecules. (Refer to Figure 3.)

Key Science Concepts

- polymers and their properties
- product development and testing

Cross-Curricular Integration

Language Arts
Design a use for polyethylene film that utilizes its directional strength. Use this idea in a story or advertisement.

Mathematics
Determine a class average for the mass of water required to break the strips in the lengthwise orientation and the widthwise orientation.

Social Studies
Conduct a survey of students' homes to see how many plastic items are in their homes. Then, have students ask parents or grandparents about how plastic has changed the way their families live.

Have students investigate the roles that polyethylene played in World War II, in the hula hoop craze, and in disposable diapers in the 1970s and 1980s.

References

Becker, R. "Teflon Tape," *Chem 13 News.* 1994, 234, 8.

Shellhammer, G., Lake View, OH, personal communication.

Water-Soluble Plastics

In a hospital, what kind of material would you use to transfer highly contaminated linens to the laundry? A water-soluble plastic called polyvinyl alcohol is used to make laundry bags for hospitals. These bags protect the hospital staff and dissolve in the wash. In this activity, students test the solubility of polyvinyl alcohol in water baths of different temperatures.

Recommended Grade Level **9–12**
Group Size .... **1–4 students**
Time for Preparation .... **30–50 minutes (+1 night drying time)**
Time for Procedure .... **40 minutes**

Materials

Procedure

Per Group
- 4 150-mL beakers
- 4 2.5-cm x 2.5-cm (1-in x 1-in) pieces of polyvinyl alcohol film prepared from 4% polyvinyl alcohol solution as described in Getting Ready
- 4 2.5-cm x 2.5-cm (1-in x 1-in) pieces of a water-soluble laundry bag
- alcohol or metal thermometer
- stirring rod
- timing device with a second hand
- goggles

Per Class
- 4% polyvinyl alcohol solution purchased or made using the following:
  - 40 g (⅓ cup) hydrolyzed, granular polyvinyl alcohol
  - 1 L water
  - hot plate or access to a full-size microwave oven
  - stirring rod
  - large glass container
- hot plate or Bunsen burner, ring stand, and wire gauze
- plastic petri dishes or aluminum or glass pie pans

Variations
- soap and detergent solutions
- white glue

Resources

Polyvinyl alcohol powder or 4% polyvinyl alcohol solution can be purchased from a chemical supply company such as Flinn Scientific, P.O. Box 219, Batavia, IL 60510-0219, 800/452-1261.

- polyvinyl alcohol powder—catalog # P0153 for 100 g
- 4% polyvinyl alcohol solution—catalog # P0210 for 1 L

Water-soluble laundry bags can be purchased and mail-ordered from certain paper companies such as Buhler Paper (also known as Bunzl Paper), 4699 Malsbary Road, Cincinnati, OH 45242, 513/253-4481. Other suppliers can be found by calling a hospital or health-care facility.

Safety and Disposal

Goggles should be worn when performing this activity. Because of the potential breakage of thermometers, alcohol or metal cooking thermometers should be used.

Getting Ready

1. If a 4% polyvinyl alcohol solution is not purchased, a solution of this approximate concentration can be prepared using one of the following methods:

   a. Dissolve 40 g (⅓ cup) 99% hydrolyzed, granular polyvinyl alcohol in 1 L water while stirring. Heat the mixture on a hot plate over moderately-high heat, stirring constantly. The solution will initially be quite milky in color, but will clear when the polyvinyl alcohol is completely dissolved. The process may take 30–45 minutes. Cool the solution before using. If a slimy or gooey layer appears on the top during cooling, simply skim it off and discard.

   b. Dissolve 40 g (⅓ cup) 99% hydrolyzed granular polyvinyl alcohol in 1 L water in a large glass container. Stir the solution and place it into a full-size microwave oven. Heat the solution on high for 8–10 minutes, stirring every 2 minutes. Do not attempt to make more than 1 L at a time.

2. One day before the lab, prepare the polyvinyl alcohol film by pouring a thin layer of 4% polyvinyl alcohol solution into a pie pan or into several plastic petri dishes. The film will dry overnight and easily peel out of the pan or dish.

Opening Strategy

Show students a water-soluble polyvinyl alcohol laundry bag and explain what it is used for and why. Ask them how they might test the solubility of the material.

Procedure

1. Pour about 50 mL water at each of the following temperatures into a different 150-mL beaker:
   - room-temperature water
   - hot tap water (about 40°C)
   - 60–70°C water
   - boiling water (100°C)

2. Determine and record the temperature of the water in each of the containers.

3. Place equal-sized pieces (about 2.5 cm x 2.5 cm, 1 in x 1 in) of the polyvinyl alcohol film (made in Getting Ready) and the water-soluble laundry bag into each beaker. Stir. Note any changes in each sample and record the time it takes for the changes to occur. Discard the remains of each sample in the trash.

 Polyvinyl alcohol will not completely dissolve in the water even at the hottest temperature. It turns to a gelatinous mass which eventually breaks up.

Variations

- Test the solubility of the laundry bags in soap and detergent solutions at various temperatures.

- Vary the thickness of the film by pouring the polyvinyl alcohol to different depths in Getting Ready. Compare the rate of solubility.

- Make white glue polymer film by pouring the glue into a thin layer in an aluminum pan. Allow it to dry. Test the film in various temperatures of water.

Discussion

- Ask students what effect temperature has on the solubility of the polyvinyl alcohol film. *As the temperature increases, the polyvinyl alcohol dissolves more quickly in water.*

- Ask students to think of other applications of water-soluble plastics.

Explanation

Most polymer films made of polyethylene (used in sandwich and trash bags) or polyvinyl chloride (used in umbrellas, raincoats, and shower curtains) are very flexible, strong, and water-resistant. This last quality makes these polymers very versatile and practical. But there seems to be a growing need for polymers that lack this characteristic. Scientists are finding more and more uses for water-soluble polymers.

The water-soluble laundry bags are made of polyvinyl alcohol. The repeating unit in this polymer is shown in Figure 1.

$$\left[\begin{array}{c} \overset{\displaystyle H}{\underset{\displaystyle H}{|}} \ \overset{\displaystyle H}{\underset{\displaystyle OH}{|}} \\ -C-C- \end{array}\right]_n$$

Figure 1: The repeating unit of polyvinyl alcohol

The numerous alcohol groups (–OH) on the giant molecule are attracted to water. The dotted lines in Figure 2 provide a graphic illustration of this attraction which is called hydrogen bonding. Alcohols of much smaller molecular weights, such as methyl alcohol (CH_3OH) or ethyl alcohol (CH_3CH_2OH), are readily soluble in water in all proportions. Polyvinyl alcohol is much less soluble in water than these two low-molecular-weight alcohols because of its sheer size. However, the large number of –OH groups (Every other carbon on the chain has an –OH group) provides the necessary attraction for polyvinyl alcohol to be soluble in hot water. The polyvinyl alcohol first tends to form a gel as it traps water molecules in its complex, interwoven structure. The amount of surface area of the polyvinyl alcohol sample and the temperature of the water both greatly affect polyvinyl alcohol's solubility.

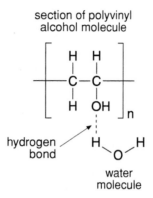

Figure 2: Attraction between water and polyvinyl alcohol

In industry, polyvinyl alcohol can be made into a film by spreading a solution of polyvinyl alcohol onto a flat, moving belt. (See Figure 3.) A blade spreads the solution uniformly and controls the thickness. The moving belt carries the solution through a drying oven, where the excess water evaporates and the material dries to a colorless solid. After cooling, the film is peeled from the belt and rolled for shipment. Uses of polyvinyl alcohol films range from laundry bags and detergent containers to pesticide and herbicide containers. The polyvinyl alcohol film keeps the farmers from being exposed to the dangerous pesticides and herbicides.

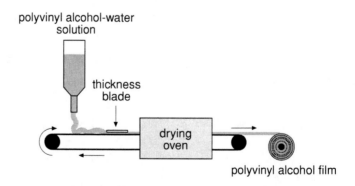

Figure 3: Process for making polyvinyl alcohol films
(Figure adapted from "Dissolving Plastics," ChemMatters.)

Key Science Concepts

- polymers and their properties
- solubility and temperature dependence

Cross-Curricular Integration

Language Arts
Have students create their own commercials for polyvinyl alcohol products and perform them for the class.

Social Studies
Discuss the history and development of polyvinyl alcohol and other related polymers.

Discuss the quantity of polyvinyl alcohol produced each year, its value to the economy as a commercial item, and its potential for growth in creating jobs and revenue.

References

Heinrich, T., Badin High School, Hamilton, Ohio, personal communication.

Wood, C.G. "Dissolving Plastics," *ChemMatters*. 1987, 5(3), 12–14.

Making a Polyester

What do you think of when you hear the word "polyester"? Leisure suits and stretch pants may come to mind, but polyesters are used in other products. In this activity students make a polyester called Glyptal®.

> Recommended Grade Level .... **9–12 as a hands-on activity**
> **4–8 as a demonstration**
> Group Size .... **1–4 students**
> Time for Preparation .... **5 minutes**
> Time for Procedure .... **15 minutes (+ 90 minutes drying time)**

Materials

Procedure

Per Group

- 2 10-cm x 10-cm (4-in x 4-in) squares of heavy-duty aluminum foil
- 50-mL beaker
- 100-mL beaker
- large disposable test tube (20-mm x 150-mm)
- stirring rod
- 10 g phthalic anhydride
- 0.5 g sodium acetate ($NaC_2H_3O_2$)
- 4 mL glycerol (glycerin)
- 1 drop red food color
- ring stand, utility clamp, and Bunsen burner
- a small object such as a coin, glass marble, or medallion
- goggles

Resources

Phthalic anhydride, sodium acetate, glycerol, and disposable test tubes can be purchased from a chemical supply company such as Flinn Scientific, P.O. Box 219, Batavia, IL 60510-0219, 800/452-1261.

- phthalic anhydride—catalog # P0028 for 500 g
- sodium acetate—catalog # S0036 for 100 g
- glycerol—catalog # G0007 for 500 mL
- 20-mm x 150-mm disposable test tubes—catalog # GP7041 for 250

Glycerol can also be purchased at a pharmacy or grocery store.

Safety and Disposal

Goggles should be worn when performing this activity. Phthalic anhydride is toxic if ingested and is a skin and respiratory irritant. If contact with the skin or eyes is made, rinse thoroughly with water for 15 minutes. Seek medical attention while the rinsing is occurring. Glycerol can cause allergic skin and eye irritation in some people. If contact is made with the skin or eyes, wash thoroughly with water.

It is highly recommended that disposable test tubes be used for this activity. The used disposable test tubes should be discarded in the trash at the end of the activity.

If you choose to use regular test tubes, clean them with an organic solvent such as acetone or hexane since Glyptal is only soluble in organic solvents. Hexane and acetone are very flammable; keep them away from open flames. Both liquids are toxic if ingested. Vapors of both compounds are irritating to the respiratory system, and hexane vapor, in high concentrations, can be narcotic. Use hexane and acetone only in a fume hood or other well-ventilated area.

Opening Strategy

The type of reaction which occurs in the synthesis of Glyptal is classified as a condensation polymerization reaction. This type of polymerization reaction between phthalic anhydride and glycerol can be visualized with a kinesthetic demonstration. (See Kinesthetic Demonstrations in Using the Activities in the Classroom.)

Procedure

1. Construct a sturdy, double-layered, aluminum-foil cup by pressing the foil squares around the outside of a 50-mL beaker. Remove the beaker and place only the aluminum cup inside a 100-mL beaker.

2. Weigh out 10 g phthalic anhydride and pour it into a large disposable test tube. Weigh out 0.5 g sodium acetate ($NaC_2H_3O_2$) and add it to the test tube. Mix well with a stirring rod.

3. Add 4 mL glycerol and one drop of red food color to the test tube. Mix well.

4. Clamp the tube (near its top) to a ring stand and adjust the angle of the tube to approximately 45°.

While heating the test tube in the following steps, be sure that the open end of the test tube is pointed away from yourself and others.

5. Heat the test tube with a moderately cool flame. To avoid local overheating, use continuous sweeping strokes over the bottom ⅓ of the test tube. After 5–6 minutes, observe as the mixture becomes clear and a slight color change (from red to yellow) occurs. After the color change occurs, continue heating for 3 more minutes.

The liquid in the test tube is very hot. Care should be taken to avoid burning yourself.

6. Turn off the heat and, using the clamp as a test tube holder, carefully pour the hot contents of the test tube into the aluminum foil mold.

7. Insert a small object (coin, medallion, etc.) into the polymer and allow the polymer to cool slowly to room temperature.

8. Allow the polymer to cure for at least 90 minutes, and then remove it from the mold by gently peeling away the aluminum foil. Examine the polymer. (It should be hard and possibly a little sticky.)

9. (optional) Test the resulting polymer for various properties such as hardness, scratch resistance, and/or solubility in different solvents (e.g., water, fingernail polish remover).

Discussion

- Glyptal is a condensation polymer. Show students the formulas for the starting materials and tell them that water is the by-product of the reaction. From this information, ask them to suggest a formula for the resulting polymer.
  See the Explanation.

- Ask students what happens to the water produced in the reaction.
  Due to heating, the water becomes vapor and escapes.

Explanation

Polymers are made up of many repeating units called monomers. In polyester polymers, the monomer units are linked by ester linkages. The existence of many ester bonds gives these polymers their name, polyester. Glyptal is a polyester resin which can be added to latex paints to improve washability and adhesion or can be used as an embedding resin as in this activity. A synthetic resin, like Glyptal, is defined as a synthetic polymer formed by the reaction of two or more substances, usually with heat or a catalyst. Resins are different from plastics. A resin is the pure or native polymer itself; a plastic is the polymer plus fillers and additives. One of the outstanding characteristics of polyesters is their ability to cure or harden at room temperature under little or no pressure. Some polyesters can also be formed into fibers and woven into cloth.

Ester formation typically results from the dehydration-condensation reaction between a carboxylic acid (–COOH) and an alcohol (–OH). (See Figure 1.)

a. general reaction:

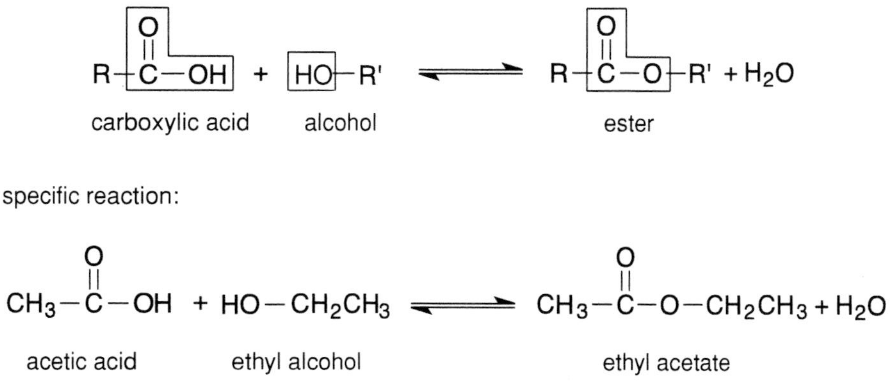

$$R-\overset{\overset{\displaystyle O}{\|}}{C}-OH \ + \ HO-R' \ \rightleftharpoons \ R-\overset{\overset{\displaystyle O}{\|}}{C}-O-R' + H_2O$$

carboxylic acid   alcohol   ester

b. specific reaction:

$$CH_3-\overset{\overset{\displaystyle O}{\|}}{C}-OH \ + \ HO-CH_2CH_3 \ \rightleftharpoons \ CH_3-\overset{\overset{\displaystyle O}{\|}}{C}-O-CH_2CH_3 + H_2O$$

acetic acid   ethyl alcohol   ethyl acetate

Figure 1: The reaction resulting in the formation of an ester linkage

In this activity, Glyptal is formed by the reaction of phthalic anhydride and glycerol. Phthalic anhydride is an acid anhydride—two carboxylic acids which have had a water molecule removed. Glycerol is a trialcohol. This combination of functional groups allows a three-dimensional network of ester linkages to form. The reaction is shown in Figure 2. Such three-dimensional networks are typically more rigid than linear polymers. This rigidity helps give Glyptal its durability, making it a useful component of paints and coatings. The three-dimensional network also makes Glyptal a thermoset polymer. Once set, thermoset polymers harden into a form which will not melt upon heating.

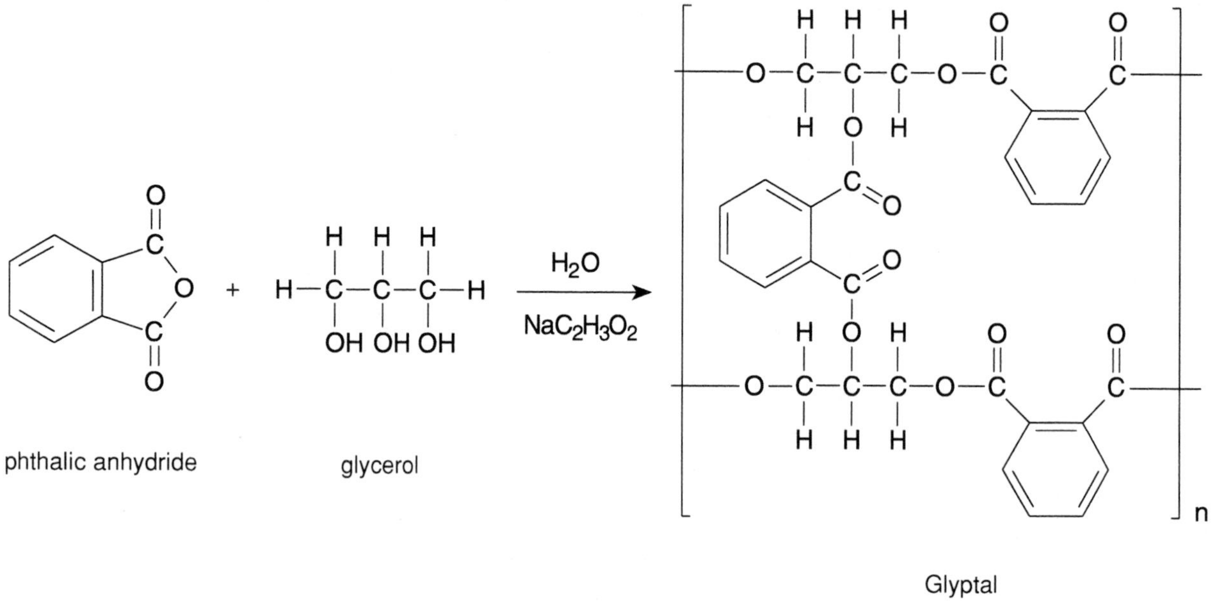

Figure 2: The formation of Glyptal

Key Science Concepts

- condensation polymerization
- dehydration
- thermoset polymer
- polymers and their properties

Cross-Curricular Integration

Language Arts
Explore the present-day connotations of several polymer terms such as plastic, polyester, nylon, and vinyl. Have students construct a survey to determine if these terms have positive, negative, or neutral connotations and if the age of the consumer impacts on the results.

Social Studies
Have students research the meaning of the "plastics revolution."

References

Armstrong; et al. *Laboratory Chemistry: A Life Science Approach;* Macmillan: New York, 1980.

Lipscomb, R. *Polymer Chemistry;* National Science Teachers Association: Washington, D.C., 1989.

Nylon 6-10

Where do synthetic fabrics come from? In this activity students see how one synthetic fiber, nylon, is made by bringing together two chemical compounds. This type of nylon (nylon 6-10) forms at the boundary of the two chemicals and can be pulled into a thread that can be wound around a stick or stretched across a room and down a hallway. See how long a thread you can make from one batch. A thread over 10 m long can be produced from 25 mL of each solution.

Recommended Grade Level **9–12**
Group Size .... **demonstration**
Time for Preparation .... **none**
Time for Procedure .... **10 minutes**

Materials

Procedure

Per Class
- 5–15 mL (1–3 tsp) 0.5 M hexamethylenediamine solution in a 0.5 M sodium hydroxide solution
- 5–15 mL (1–3 tsp) 0.2 M sebacoyl chloride solution in hexane
- water
- (optional) food color
- rubbing alcohol (70% isopropyl alcohol solution)
- 50-mL or 100-mL beaker
- forceps or tweezers
- stirring stick, glass rod, or test tube
- plastic or rubber gloves
- goggles

Resources

The 0.5 M hexamethylenediamine solution in a 0.5 M sodium hydroxide solution and the 0.2 M sebacoyl chloride solution in hexane are available from a chemical supply company such as Flinn Scientific, P.O. Box 219, Batavia, IL 60510-0219, 800/452-1261.

- hexamethylenediamine/sodium hydroxide solution—catalog # H0032 for 100 mL
- sebacoyl chloride/hexane solution—catalog # S0260 for 100 mL

Safety and Disposal

Goggles should be worn when performing this activity. Hexamethylenediamine and sebacoyl chloride are irritating to the skin, eyes, and respiratory system. Inhalation or contact with skin and eyes must be prevented. Gloves are recommended when handling these compounds. In addition, hexamethylenediamine has a strong, unpleasant fishy odor.

Dilute solutions of sodium hydroxide (NaOH) are caustic and can cause serious chemical burns. Handle this solution with care to avoid skin and eye contact. Should contact occur, rinse the affected area. If the contact involves the eyes, medical attention should be sought while the rinsing is occurring. The unused sodium hydroxide solution can be saved for future use or diluted with water and flushed down the drain.

Hexane vapor can irritate the respiratory tract and, in high concentrations, can be narcotic. In addition, hexane is extremely flammable. Use it in a well-ventilated room.

After the demonstration, any reactants remaining in the reaction beaker should be mixed thoroughly using a stirring stick or stirring rod to produce nylon. Remove the nylon, wash it with water, then discard it in a solid waste container. Any remaining liquid should be rinsed down the drain with large amounts of water. Unused portions of the solutions can be stored in tightly capped bottles for later use.

 Avoid storing solutions in bottles with ground glass stoppers as they may become sealed shut by the reagents.

Procedure

1. Wearing gloves to protect your hands, pour about 5–15 mL (1–3 tsp) hexamethylenediamine/sodium hydroxide solution into a 50-mL or 100-mL beaker.

2. (optional) Add 1–5 drops of food color to the hexamethylenediamine/ sodium hydroxide solution to make the nylon more visible.

3. Slowly pour an equal amount (5–15 mL as in Step 1) of the sebacoyl chloride/hexane solution down the side of the beaker onto the hexamethylenediamine/sodium hydroxide solution. Take care not to mix the two solutions. The sebacoyl chloride solution should form a discrete layer over the first solution. A distinct boundary will be visible between the solutions.

4. A film of nylon will form at the interface of the two solutions. Grasp the film with forceps or tweezers and pull it up slowly from the center of the beaker. Take care to keep the nylon rope from touching the sides of the beaker. (Otherwise, the rope may snag and break.) This is best accomplished by pulling the thread straight up from the center of the beaker.

5. Wind the nylon around the center of the stirring stick, glass rod, or test tube. Continue to do so until the rope eventually breaks or one of the two reagents is used up. The forceps or tweezers can be used to guide the progress of the thread.

6. Leave the nylon on the stick or tube and immerse it in water, swirling it to help wash it. Repeat the procedure with rubbing alcohol and again with water before handling. (If food color has been added it will wash out in this process.)

7. Be sure you still have your gloves on when handling the fiber, as unreacted reagents may still be present. Experiment with the nylon fiber. Does it stretch? Is it elastic?

Discussion

- Show students the equation for the condensation polymerization of nylon. (See Figure 1.) Challenge them to explain where the hydrochloric acid (HCl), which is formed as a by-product, went.
  The sodium hydroxide solution (NaOH) reacts with hydrochloric acid to neutralize the hydrochloric acid.

- Discuss why nylon might be the fabric of choice for such items as carpet, parachutes, jogging suits, and windbreakers.
  Nylon is lightweight; nylon fibers are very strong; and nylon fabric, when coated, is water-repellent.

Explanation

Nylon was first developed at DuPont as a synthetic replacement for silk. Many different forms of nylon have been made by combining a molecule that has two amine ($-NH_2$) groups (diamine) with a molecule that has two acid ($-COOH$) groups (diacid) or two acid chloride groups (COCl). The various nylons produced are named using a system which indicates the number of carbon atoms in the diamine and the acid. In this activity, nylon 6-10 is made from hexamethylenediamine (6 carbon atoms) and sebacoyl chloride (10 carbon atoms). This reaction is illustrated in Figure 1.

$$H_2N(CH_2)_6NH_2 \ + \ Cl-\overset{\overset{O}{\|}}{C}-(CH_2)_8-\overset{\overset{O}{\|}}{C}-Cl \ \longrightarrow \ \left[-\overset{\overset{H}{|}}{N}(CH_2)_6\overset{\overset{H}{|}}{N}-\overset{\overset{O}{\|}}{C}(CH_2)_8\overset{\overset{O}{\|}}{C}-\right]_n \ + \ 2HCl$$

| hexamethylene-diamine | sebacoyl chloride | Nylon 6-10 | hydrochloric acid |

Figure 1: The formation of Nylon 6-10

The preparation of nylon is a condensation polymerization reaction. This type of polymerization reaction between hexamethylenediamine and sebacoyl chloride can be visualized with a kinesthetic demonstration. (See Kinesthetic Demonstrations in Using the Activities in the Classroom.)

The hexamethylenediamine is dissolved in an aqueous 0.5 M sodium hydroxide (NaOH) solution and the sebacoyl chloride is dissolved in hexane. During the polymerization process, the by-product hydrochloric acid (HCl), which is insoluble in hexane, dissolves into the aqueous phase where it reacts with the sodium hydroxide and is neutralized according to the equation shown in Figure 2.

$$HCl \ + \ NaOH \ \longrightarrow \ NaCl \ + \ H_2O$$

| hydrochloric acid | sodium hydroxide | sodium chloride | water |

Figure 2: The neutralization of hydrochloric acid by sodium hydroxide

Nylon threads are processed for use in fabrics, rope, or monofilament line by cold drawing. The cold drawing process is similar to what was done in the activity when the film was pulled from the boundary so that it formed a strand. The film that forms when the two chemicals combine is not very strong. However, when stretched, the polymer chains line up in parallel rows. This allows the oxygen atoms on one strand to form hydrogen bonds with the hydrogen atoms on adjacent strands. In this way the nylon polymers become much stronger, just as individual strands of wire combine to form a strong cable. (See Figure 3.)

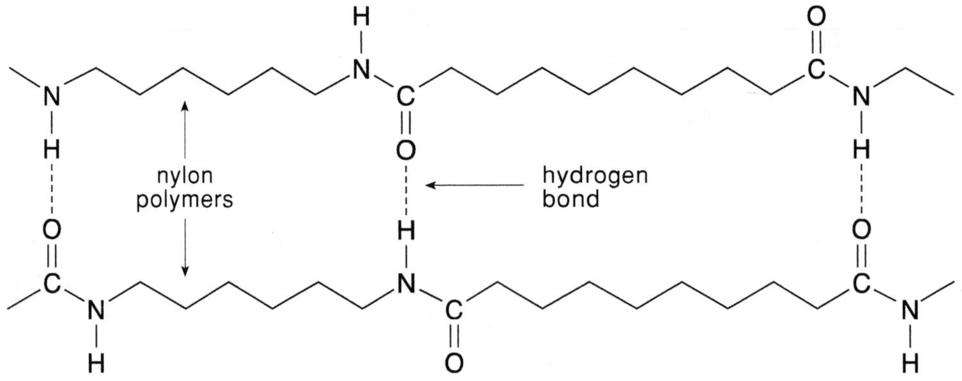

Figure 3: The hydrogen bonding between Nylon 6-10 strands

Key Science Concepts

- acid/base neutralization
- condensation polymerization
- industrial processes
- polymers and their properties

Cross-Curricular Integration

Social Studies
Discuss the impact that synthetic polymers (such as nylon and polyester) have had on society.

Research the history of nylon use in hosiery.

References

"Nylon 6-10;" *Fun With Chemistry: A Guidebook of K–12 Activities;* Sarquis, M., Sarquis, J., Eds.; Institute for Chemical Education: Madison, WI, 1991; Vol. 1, pp 217–220.

Shakhashiri, B.Z. *Chemical Demonstrations;* University of Wisconsin: Madison, WI, 1983; Vol. 1, pp 213–215.

Making Polyvinyl Alcohol Fibers ![8]

How can you produce a threadlike fiber from two liquids? Is it magic? No, it's science. Try this activity and see.

Recommended Grade Level 7–12
Group Size .... demonstration or groups of 1–4 students
Time for Preparation .... 0–30 minutes
Time for Procedure .... 10–15 minutes (+ overnight for drying)

Materials

Procedure

Per Group or Class

- 50 mL 4% polyvinyl alcohol solution purchased or made as described in Getting Ready
- 50 mL acetone
- 150-mL beaker
- forceps or tweezers
- stirring rod or plastic spoon
- 30-cm x 30-cm piece of aluminum foil
- aluminum pie pan
- (optional) food color
- goggles

Variation

- 50 mL 4% polyvinyl alcohol solution
- 10-mL or larger plastic syringe
- beaker of acetone
- plastic petri dish
- aluminum foil or paper towel
- overhead projector
- tweezers or forceps

Resources

The polyvinyl alcohol (as a 4% solution or granular solid) and acetone can be purchased from a chemical supply company such as Flinn Scientific, P.O. Box 219, Batavia, IL, 60510-0219, 800/452-1261.

- 4% polyvinyl alcohol solution—catalog # P0209 for 500 mL
- 99% hydrolyzed, granular polyvinyl alcohol (minimum molecular weight of 100,000)— catalog # P0153 for 100 g
- acetone—catalog # A0009 for 500 mL

Acetone can also be purchased at a hardware store.

Safety and Disposal

Goggles must be worn when performing this activity. Acetone is very flammable. Keep the acetone away from flames and heat, which could cause it to ignite. Acetone vapors are irritating to the eyes and respiratory system, and the liquid is toxic if ingested. Use acetone only in a well-ventilated area. Acetone may be discarded down the drain with large amounts of water.

Polyvinyl alcohol fibers may be discarded in the trash.

Getting Ready

If 4% polyvinyl alcohol solution is not purchased, you can prepare a solution of this approximate concentration using one of the following methods:

a. Dissolve 40 g (⅓ cup) 99% hydrolyzed, granular polyvinyl alcohol in 1 L water while stirring. Heat the mixture on a hot plate over moderately-high heat, stirring constantly. The solution will initially be quite milky in color, but will clear when the polyvinyl alcohol is completely dissolved. The process may take up to 30–45 minutes. Cool the solution before using. If a slimy or gooey layer appears on the top during cooling, skim it off and discard.

b. Alternatively, dissolve 40 g (⅓ cup) 99% hydrolyzed granular polyvinyl alcohol in 1 L water in a large glass container. Stir the solution and place it into a full-size microwave oven. Heat the solution on high for 8–10 minutes, stirring every 2 minutes. Do not attempt to make more than 1 L at a time.

Procedure

1. Pour about 50 mL 4% polyvinyl alcohol solution into a 150-mL beaker so that the depth of the solution is approximately 2 cm.

2. (optional) Add a drop of food color and mix well with a stirring rod or plastic spoon.

3. Tip the beaker slightly and pour in an equal depth of acetone (about 50 mL). The acetone will form a layer on top of the polyvinyl alcohol solution. Immediately after adding the acetone, a thin, white interface of polyvinyl alcohol forms between the two layers. (See Figure 1.)

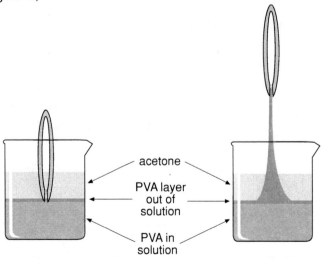

Figure 1: The setup for producing polyvinyl alcohol fibers

4. As shown in Figure 1, pick up the interface layer using a pair of forceps or tweezers and pull it slowly straight upward out of the beaker. Usually a strand about 40–60 cm long can be pulled out.

5. Lay the strand on the aluminum foil to dry. Many such strands can be pulled out of the beaker before the polyvinyl alcohol layer is exhausted.

6. Pour enough of the 4% polyvinyl alcohol solution into an aluminum pie pan to cover the bottom. This solution will form a film over the bottom of the pan.

7. Allow the fibers and film in the aluminum pan to dry overnight. During the next class period, test the stretchability of one of the polyvinyl alcohol fibers and of a piece of the polyvinyl alcohol film cut from the larger piece of film. Record any observations.

8. Dip pieces of both the polyvinyl alcohol fiber and film into a container of water once or twice and then repeat the stretchability test. Record any observations.

Variation

- Polyvinyl alcohol fibers can also be made by filling a 10-mL plastic syringe with the polyvinyl alcohol solution and slowly extruding it through the tip into a petri dish of acetone on an overhead projector. The 20-cm fiber can be removed after a few seconds with a pair of tweezers and placed in a beaker of acetone to harden for a few minutes. The fibers can be dried with a paper towel and used for later experiments.

Discussion

- Discuss the fact that this is not a polymerization reaction, but rather a drying of the strand of polyvinyl alcohol as it is pulled from the aqueous solution through the acetone. *When polyvinyl alcohol is dissolved in water, water molecules become associated with the polyvinyl alcohol polymer chains. The acetone strips these water molecules away from the polyvinyl alcohol chains, forming dehydrated strands of polyvinyl alcohol polymer.*

- Ask the students to compare the properties of the polyvinyl alcohol fibers to the polyvinyl alcohol film.
  When dry, the dehydrated strands of polyvinyl alcohol fiber or the film will not stretch and may break. If the film and the fibers are placed in water, both the fibers and the film become stretchy.

Explanation

The polyvinyl alcohol solution used in this activity contains long polymer chains of polyvinyl alcohol that are dissolved in water. The length of the polymer chains and the hydrogen bonding that exists between the chains causes the solution to be rather thick or viscous and to pour more slowly than water.

While soluble in water, the polyvinyl alcohol polymer is not soluble in acetone. The acetone can be termed a non-solvent and removes the water from the polyvinyl alcohol that passes through it. This results in strands of polyvinyl alcohol being pulled from the interface of the acetone-polyvinyl alcohol boundary. When dry, the strands have some flexibility, but are inelastic. If dipped briefly in water, the water associates with the polymer, providing elasticity to the strand. This is also true for the polyvinyl alcohol films. When dry, the film is also not elastic, but will stretch after soaking in water for a few seconds.

Key Science Concepts

- polymers and their properties
- solubility

Cross-Curricular Integration

Home, Safety, and Career
Read the labels of some common hairstyling gels and face-mask gels to determine if they contain polyvinyl alcohol. Discuss reasons why polyvinyl alcohol might be included in such products.

Social Studies
Discuss the impact synthetic polymers (e.g., nylon, polyester, etc.) have had on society.

References

Casassa, E.Z.; Sarquis, A.M.; Van Dyke, C.H. "The Gelation of Polyvinyl Alcohol with Borax," *Journal of Chemical Education*. 1986, 63, 57.

Morgan, P.W.; Kwolek, S.L. "The Nylon Rope Trick," *Journal of Chemical Education*. 1959, 36, 182, 530.

Rodriguez, F. "Classroom Demonstrations of Polymer Principles Part V: Polymer Fabrication," *Journal of Chemical Education*. 1992, 69, 915–920.

Sherman, M.C. "Producing Fibers of Poly(vinyl alcohol)," *Journal of Chemical Education*. 1992, 69, 883.

Comparison of Paper, Polyethylene, and Tyvek

9

How do different kinds of polymers compare in terms of strength, flexibility, and water resistance? In this activity students compare the properties of three polymers: cellulose, a natural polymer that is used to make paper; polyethylene film, a synthetic polymer; and Tyvek®, a nonwoven fabric made from polyethylene fibers.

Recommended Grade Level 4–12
Group Size .... 1–4 students
Time for Preparation .... none
Time for Procedure .... Part 1: 10 minutes
　　　　　　　　　　　　　　　　　Part 2: 15 minutes (+ 5 minutes per day for 3–5 days)

Materials

Procedure, Part 1
Per Group
- 10-cm x 10-cm (4-in x 4-in) square of each of the following:
    - paper
    - low-density polyethylene film (sandwich bag or dry-cleaning bag)
    - Tyvek (computer-disk sleeve or express-mail envelope)
- container of water
- sharp pen or pencil

Procedure, Part 2
- 10-cm x 10-cm (4-in x 4-in) square of the following:
    - paper
    - polyethylene film
    - Tyvek
- 3 transparent plastic cups
- modeling clay
- permanent marker or grease pencil
- sharp scissors
- graduated cylinder or tablespoon

Procedure

Part 1: Comparing Strength
Conduct each of the following tests on the squares of paper, polyethylene film, and Tyvek and record your results.

1. Determine the comparative strengths of each polymer by trying to tear each sample.

2. Determine the flexibility of each polymer by bending each sample in the same place repeatedly.

Chain Gang—The Chemistry of Polymers　　　　77　　　　Comparison of Paper, Polyethylene, and Tyvek

3. Determine the puncture resistance of each polymer by pushing the tip of a pen or sharp pencil through each sample.

4. Determine the water resistance of each polymer by soaking a piece of each sample in water and shaking off the excess water.

Part 2: Comparing Permeability

Perform the following procedure with a new sample of each material.

1. Trace the cup rim onto each polymer sample. Use sharp scissors to cut out the circle.

2. Pour exactly 30 mL (2 Tbsp) water into the cup.

3. Use rings of modeling clay to seal the polymer circle over the cup. (See Figure 1.)

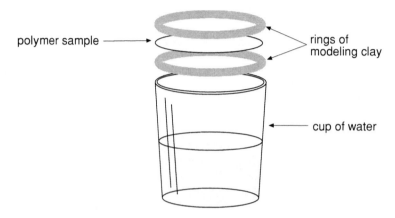

Figure 1: Arrangement of modeling clay and polymer circle

4. Mark the water levels on the cups with a marker or grease pencil, and then place them in a warm spot.

5. Observe and record the water level in each glass over a period of several days. Compare the rate of evaporation of water through the different materials and record these observations.

Extension

- In order to choose a material to make a product from, product engineers need to know the precise rate of vapor passage in grams of water per hour per square meter (g/hr•m²) of material. Design an experiment that would allow you to determine this rate for paper, polyethylene, and Tyvek.

  Possible Experiment: Control the surface area of each sample, temperature, and time so that they are the same for each sample. Measure the amount of water in milliliters lost over a set time period. Calculate the rate according to the following equation:

$$rate = (mL\ H_2O\ (l)\ lost) \left(\frac{1g\ H_2O\ (l)}{1\ mL\ H_2O\ (l)} \right) \left(\frac{1}{area\ in\ m^2} \right) \left(\frac{1}{time\ in\ hr} \right)$$

Discussion

- Discuss the results from the tests performed in Part 1 for the three polymers used in this activity.
  See Table 1.

Table 1: Comparison of the Properties of Paper, Low-Density Polyethylene, and Tyvek

Material	Strength	Flexibility	Puncture Resistance	Water Resistance
paper	easily torn	flexible	can be punctured	not water-resistant
low-density polyethylene	tears with effort	flexible	can be punctured	water-resistant
Tyvek	does not tear	flexible	does not puncture	water-resistant

- Ask students which of the three polymers permitted the greatest permeability of water and which of the three allowed the least permeability of water. Discuss reasons for these findings.
  Tyvek and paper both allowed about the same amount of water evaporation; the polyethylene allowed the least amount of evaporation. Some reasons for these observations are that the polyethylene polymer chains are packed closely together in the film and will not allow water vapor to penetrate; Tyvek and paper, on the other hand, have openings in the molecular structure which allow the water vapor to penetrate.

Explanation

In Part 1, it was shown that Tyvek is exceptionally strong as compared to paper and low-density polyethylene film. The Tyvek can be flexed thousands of times without breaking. Water will run off of Tyvek and polyethylene films or lie in drops on the surface, but paper absorbs water. Tyvek is water-resistant because although there are air spaces in it, these spaces wind around and between the tiny fibers and keep the water from penetrating the film. Polyethylene film is water-resistant due to the close packing of the polymer chains—no water molecules can penetrate this barrier.

In Part 2 of the activity, polyethylene film had the smallest amount of water loss. Again, this is due to the close packing of the polymer chains which does not allow the water to penetrate the film. Unlike polyethylene, Tyvek and paper will allow water vapor and other gases to slowly pass through.

The properties of a polymer determine its uses. Cellulose, a natural polymer and the most abundant organic substance on earth, is the main ingredient in paper. It is a polysaccharide (complex carbohydrate) formed from repeating glucose units. (See Figure 2.)

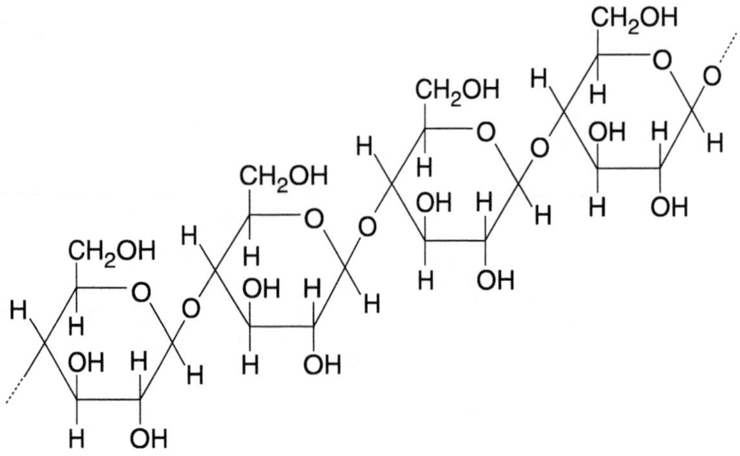

Figure 2: The structure of cellulose

Polyethylene is a synthetic polymer made up of long carbon chains. It is a very stable plastic, unreactive to acids and bases, and is waterproof. It is used to make plastic bags, frozen food packaging, shrink wrapping, meat packaging, and liquid food and chemical containers, as well as other molded items. Depending on the degree of branching of the chain that results during its preparation, polyethylene can be made in different densities which can be broadly defined as low-density polyethylene (LDPE) and high-density polyethylene (HDPE). The more branching within the polymer structure, the more flexible the plastic is. LDPE, which is a highly branched form of polyethylene, is used mainly in plastic films and bags where flexibility is more important than strength. HDPE, a form of polyethylene with little to no branching, is used for containers such as milk jugs which must remain fairly rigid.

Tyvek is a special form of HDPE. The polyethylene used in Tyvek is first formed into extremely fine fibers. These fibers are then allowed to fall randomly onto a flat moving belt. The resulting web of fibers is exposed to heat and pressure, and the fibers are melted together. If most of the fibers are fused, the material is stiff and paper-like. If only a few are joined, a softer, more cloth-like material is formed. Some of the current uses for Tyvek are mailing envelopes, computer disk sleeves, tags, labels, signs, banners, and draft-proof wrapping for houses (under siding).

Key Science Concepts

- polymers and their properties
- water permeability

Cross-Curricular Integration

Earth Science
Discuss the possibility of recycling each of the polymers used in this activity and the biodegradability of each.

Reference

Sheinberg, S.P., "Tyvek," *ChemMatters*. April 1986, 4(2), 8–10.

Producing Ethylene from Common Materials

10

In this activity, ethylene, a colorless, odorless gas, is produced from two different materials, polyethylene (used to make plastic sandwich bags or milk jugs) and paraffin oil (mineral oil).

Recommended Grade Level .... 10–12 as a hands-on activity
                                                                  7–9 as a demonstration
Group Size .... 1–4 students
Time for Preparation .... 15 minutes
Time for Procedure .... 60–65 minutes

Materials

Opening Strategy
- boxes of sandwich bags
- plastic grocery bags

Procedure
Per Group
- paper towel or cloth
- soap, vegetable oil, or glycerol (glycerin)
- 3 mL bromine water
- 2 large test tubes (20-mm x 150-mm) and 1-hole and solid rubber stoppers to fit
- 2 small test tubes (13-mm x 100-mm) and 1-hole and solid rubber stoppers to fit
- 50- to 60-cm length of rubber tubing
- 2 small pieces of fire-polished glass tubing (8–10 cm long)
- thin-stemmed, disposable plastic pipet
- 600-mL beaker or wide-mouthed bottle
- broken pieces of pottery (e.g., from a flower pot) small enough to fit in test tube
- Bunsen burner, ring stand, and utility clamp
- rubber gloves
- goggles

Procedure, Part 1
Per Group
- several small pieces of polyethylene that will easily fit in the bottom of a test tube, such as strips of a plastic sandwich bag or small pieces of a milk jug

Procedure, Part 2
Per Group
- 1–2 mL paraffin oil (mineral oil) or several small pieces of Parafilm®
- glass wool (fiberglass)
- gloves

For Cleanup (optional)

- concentrated sulfuric acid (18 M H_2SO_4)
- 6.0 g sodium thiosulfate ($Na_2S_2O_3$)
- 6 M sodium hydroxide solution (NaOH)

Resources

Paraffin oil (mineral oil), Parafilm, bromine water, and disposable plastic pipets can be purchased from a chemical supply company such as Flinn Scientific, P.O. Box 219, Batavia, IL 60510-0219, 800/452-1261.

- mineral oil—catalog # M0064 for 500 mL
- Parafilm—catalog # AP1500 for 1 roll
- bromine water—catalog # B0166 for 100 mL
- disposable plastic pipets—catalog # AP2253 for 20

Glass wool (fiberglass) can be purchased as angel hair at craft stores or as fiberglass insulation at hardware stores.

Safety and Disposal

Goggles must be worn when performing this activity.

Use care when heating the paraffin oil and polyethylene; the gases produced are flammable. Be sure that the stoppers fit tightly and do not leak. Use a piece of tubing long enough so that the ethylene gas is collected at least 0.5 m from the open flame.

Bromine water is irritating to the respiratory system and toxic if ingested. It can cause severe burns if contact with the skin is made. Use caution when handling this chemical. If contact with the skin occurs, rinse the affected area with running water for 10–15 minutes. Bromine water can be saved for future use or disposed of by vigorously shaking the capped bottle while wearing rubber gloves and then leaving it open in a working fume hood for several days. The bromine will escape as a gas and the remaining water (which should now be clear) can be flushed down a drain. To speed up the process, pour the bromine water into a shallow pan to increase the surface area exposed to the air.

If a fume hood is not available for disposal, the bromine water can be carefully acidified to pH 2 using concentrated sulfuric acid (18 M H_2SO_4). Prepare a solution of 6.0 g sodium thiosulfate ($Na_2S_2O_3$) in 50 mL water. Carefully add the sodium thiosulfate solution to the acidified bromine water. The brown color of the bromine water will disappear and the solution will be colorless. Neutralize the solution to pH 7 with 6 M sodium hydroxide solution, NaOH (24 g sodium hydroxide in 100 mL water), and flush the resulting solution down a drain with plenty of water.

Glass wool is very irritating to the skin. Wear gloves when handling it.

Getting Ready

1. Lubricate one end of the glass tubing with soap, vegetable oil, or glycerol. Wrap the glass in a paper towel or cloth and carefully insert the glass tubing with a twisting motion into the large 1-hole rubber stopper. (See Figure 1.)

 When inserting glass tubing into a rubber stopper, carefully follow this procedure. Glass tubing can break and cut your hand if insertion is not done carefully.

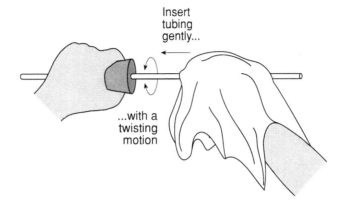

Figure 1: Inserting the glass tubing into the rubber stopper

2. Attach one end of the rubber tubing to the glass tubing that projects out of the stopper. Attach the other end of the rubber tubing to the second piece of fire-polished glass tubing. (See Figure 2.)

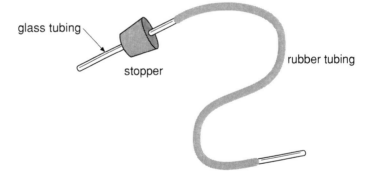

Figure 2: Attaching the rubber tubing to the pieces of glass tubing

Opening Strategy

Bring in boxes of sandwich bags and some plastic grocery bags. Read the labels and look on the bags for the composition. (Polyethylene.) Point out that milk jugs and dry-cleaning bags are also made from polyethylene. Ask the students if they know how polyethylene is made. (Polyethylene is made by polymerizing ethylene molecules.) Discuss the addition polymerization reaction of ethylene to make polyethylene.

A kinesthetic demonstration can be used to illustrate the addition polymerization reaction in which polyethylene is made from the ethylene monomer, $CH_2=CH_2$. (See Kinesthetic Demonstrations and Simulations in Using the Activities in the Classroom.)

Ethylene is a by-product of the distillation of crude oil. When crude oil is distilled, one of the components that is isolated is called naphtha. Naphtha is very similar to gasoline except that it is used as a source of chemicals (petrochemicals). Naphtha is composed of long carbon chains (5–9 carbons in the chain). These carbon chains can be broken (cracked) into smaller, more useful carbon chains. Ethylene is a product of the cracking of naphtha. Petroleum companies usually crack naphtha into other small molecules. Ask students why they think companies do this. (Petroleum companies make more money from the sales of products made from small molecules such as ethylene than they do from selling the crude oil directly. See Figure 3.)

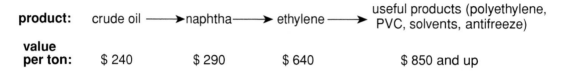

product:	crude oil ⟶	naphtha ⟶	ethylene ⟶	useful products (polyethylene, PVC, solvents, antifreeze)
value per ton:	$ 240	$ 290	$ 640	$ 850 and up

Figure 3: The increasing value of refined petroleum products

In this activity, ethylene will be produced by cracking paraffin oil (a distillation product of crude oil) and from the breakdown of polyethylene.

Procedure

> Both parts of the activity should be performed in groups or by the teacher and an assistant. It requires two or more people to manipulate the equipment in several of the steps.

Part 1: Breaking Down Polyethylene

1. Set up the apparatus as shown in Figure 4, using a utility clamp to secure a large test tube to a ring stand. Clamp the test tube near the open end.

 When setting up the apparatus and carrying out this procedure, remember that ethylene gas is flammable. Keep well away from open flames. Be sure the stoppers fit tightly and do not leak. Be sure that the collecting beaker is at least 0.5 m from the open flame.

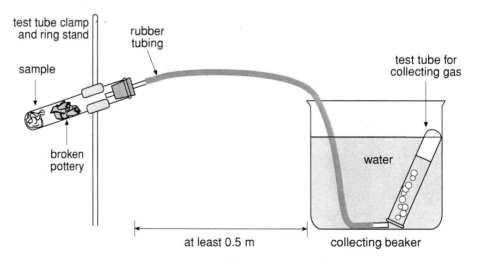

Figure 4: Apparatus for collecting ethylene gas

2. Fill one of the small test tubes with water and, holding your finger over the open end, submerge it upside down in the 600-mL beaker filled with water.

3. Place the polyethylene sample and the pottery pieces into the large test tube as shown in Figure 4.

4. Insert the stopper with the connected glass and rubber tubing (See Getting Ready) into the test tube. Place the free end of the tubing into the water as shown in Figure 4 so that the end of the rubber tubing is just beneath the small test tube.

5. With the Bunsen burner, heat the broken pottery strongly for a few minutes before gently heating the polyethylene to vaporize it. You must keep the pottery hot, so heat the polyethylene and pottery alternately. (The pottery is a catalyst for the decomposition of polyethylene molecules.)

6. As the ethylene gas is produced, bubbles will begin to appear in the collecting beaker of water. Allow the first few bubbles of gas to escape from the end of the glass or rubber tubing. Then collect one tube of gas by holding a small test tube over the end of the tubing. (If you want to determine the volume of ethylene gas produced, you will probably need several test tubes.)

Colorless, insoluble gases are typically collected over water. As the gas is generated, it displaces the water and forces it from the test tube.

If the test tube containing the sample and broken pottery is allowed to cool while the rubber tubing is still submerged, water will be quickly sucked back into the test tube.

7. Remove the end of the delivery tube from the beaker of water before you stop heating.

Bromine water can cause severe chemical burns. Handle with extreme care in the next steps. Wear gloves when using it and disposing of it. See Safety and Disposal.

8. Fill a disposable plastic pipet approximately ¼ full of bromine water.

9. While the small test tube of gas is still submerged, insert the small one-hole stopper.

10. Lift the inverted test tube from the beaker and, while keeping it in the inverted position, quickly insert the tip of the pipet into the hole in the stopper. (See Figure 5.)

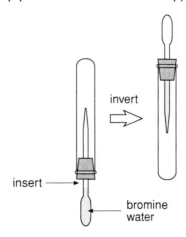

Figure 5: Adding the bromine water to the ethylene gas

11. Turn the test tube and pipet right-side-up and squeeze 20 drops (about 1 mL) bromine water into the test tube. Shake the test tube gently with the pipet still in place and note any color changes.

12. Put 2–3 small pieces of polyethylene into a clean, large test tube. With extreme caution, add 20 drops (about 1 mL) bromine water. Insert a solid stopper and shake gently. Compare the color of the bromine water to that in Step 11.

Part 2: "Cracking" the Paraffin Oil

 Ethylene gas is flammable. Keep well away from open flames. Be sure the stoppers fit tightly and do not leak. Be sure that the collecting beaker is at least 0.5 m from the open flame.

1. Repeat Steps 1 and 2 of Part 1.

2. Lightly soak a small wad of glass wool with paraffin oil, and place the soaked glass wool into the test tube. Alternatively, place a few small pieces of Parafilm in the test tube. Add the broken pottery pieces as in Part 1.

3. Repeat Part 1, Steps 4–10 to collect and test the ethylene gas.

 Bromine water can cause severe chemical burns. Handle with extreme care in the next step. Wear gloves when using it and disposing of it. See Safety and Disposal.

4. Place 40–60 drops (2–3 mL) paraffin oil into a small, clean test tube. With extreme caution, add 20 drops (about 1 mL) bromine water to the paraffin oil. Insert a solid stopper and shake gently. Compare the color of the bromine water to that in the previous step.

Discussion

- Discuss what color should result if bromine water was added to polyethylene or paraffin oil. *The bromine water, which is red-brown in color, reacts only with compounds containing carbon-carbon double bonds. Since paraffin oil and polyethylene do not contain double bonds in their molecular structure, the color should not change.*

- Ask students to propose an explanation for why the addition of bromine water to the ethylene produced a different result than its addition to the polyethylene and paraffin oil. *Ethylene must have a carbon-carbon double bond. When bromine water is added to ethylene ($CH_2=CH_2$), the bromine reacts with the ethylene. As the concentration of the bromine decreases, the red-brown color fades. The resulting yellow solution shows that the bromine has reacted with the ethylene and is no longer present in solution.*

Explanation

Polyethylene was accidentally discovered when dirty glassware acted as a catalyst for the polymerization of ethylene gas under high pressure and temperature. In the polymerization reaction, the double bond between the carbon atoms in the ethylene molecule is broken and a chain of single-bonded carbon atoms is formed. (See Figure 6.) In Part 1 of this activity, the polymerization process is reversed and the polyethylene polymer is broken down into the gaseous ethylene monomer.

$$\underset{\substack{\text{ethylene}\\\text{monomer}}}{\ce{H2C=CH2}} \xrightarrow{\text{catalyst}} \underset{\substack{\text{polyethylene}\\\text{polymer}}}{\left[\!\!\begin{array}{cccc} H & H & H & H \\ | & | & | & | \\ C & C & C & C \\ | & | & | & | \\ H & H & H & H \end{array}\!\!\right]_n}$$

Figure 6: The polymerization of ethylene

To test for the presence of ethylene, the product gas is mixed with bromine water. If ethylene, or any other double-bonded (unsaturated) carbon compound is present, it will cause the reddish-brown color of the bromine water to disappear. (See Figure 7.) Bromine does not react with carbon compounds containing only carbon-carbon single bonds (saturated compounds) such as polyethylene and paraffin.

ethylene monomer (colorless) bromine (red/brown) 1,2 dibromoethane (colorless)

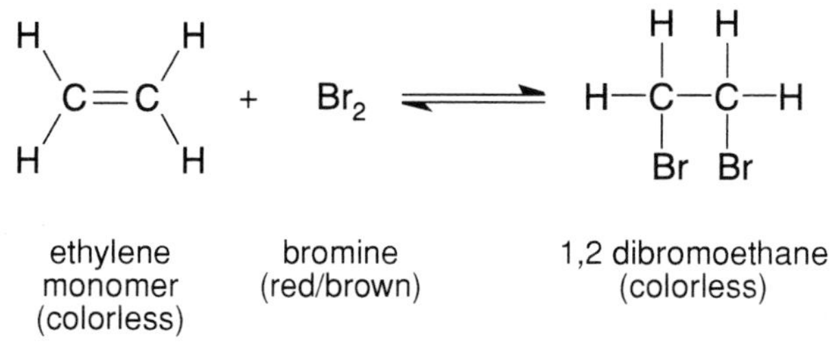

Figure 7: The reaction between bromine water and ethylene

Part 2 uses heat to break down the paraffin (a petroleum distillate) into ethylene gas, the raw material for the production of polyethylene. In the cracking process, petroleum distillates containing mixtures of hydrocarbons (usually molecules between 5–9 carbons in length) are broken down into shorter carbon-carbon chains. When hydrogen atoms are removed through dehydrogenation reactions, the resulting hydrocarbons become unsaturated. (Carbon-carbon double bonds are formed.) Ethylene is the simplest of these unsaturated hydrocarbons. (See Figure 6.) Ethylene molecules are the building blocks of complex polymers. The pieces of broken pottery act as a catalyst in this reaction by providing a surface on which the vaporized polyethylene and paraffin molecules can break down.

Key Science Concepts

- catalysts
- cracking of petroleum products
- decomposition reactions
- polymers and their properties
- saturated and unsaturated bonds

Cross-Curricular Integration

Earth Science
Outline the advantages and disadvantages of recycling polyethylene versus producing polyethylene from raw materials.

Social Studies
Discuss the variety of products made from ethylene/polyethylene and the impact that this industry has on the economy.

Reference

Plastics Unit Guide: A Fourth Year Unit for the Salters' GCSE Chemistry Course; University of York, Science Education Group: York, Great Britain, 1987.

Making Rubber Bands

In this activity, students make rubber bands and learn the chemistry behind them. They compare their rubber bands to commercially made rubber bands.

> **Recommended Grade Level** 3–12
> **Group Size** .... 1–4 students
> **Time for Preparation** .... 5 minutes
> **Time for Procedure** .... 20 minutes

Materials

Opening Strategy
- small amount of liquid latex

Procedure
Per Group
- 2 wide-mouthed, plastic cups at least 8 cm (about 3 in) high
- 60 mL (¼ cup) liquid latex
- 60 mL (¼ cup) vinegar
- sharpened pencil
- marking pen and labels
- (optional) stirring stick
- (optional) liquid tempera paint
- goggles

Variations
Per Group
- paper cup
- materials for making a super ball (See Activity 16, "Making a Super Ball.")
- plastic bottles of various shapes and sizes
- containers for latex and vinegar
- liquid latex
- stirring stick
- vinegar

Resources

Liquid latex can be purchased from a chemical supply company such as Flinn Scientific, P.O. Box 219, Batavia, IL 60510-0219, 800/452-1261.

- liquid latex—catalog # L0004 for 500 mL

Tempera paints and liquid latex under the name Pliatex Mold Rubber can be purchased from an art supply store.

Safety and Disposal

Goggles should be worn when performing this activity. Liquid latex contains ammonia as a stabilizer. Ammonia or its vapors can damage the eyes. Contact lenses should not be worn when working with ammonia-containing products as gaseous vapors of ammonia can condense on the contact lens and cause damage to the eye. Use ammonia in a well-ventilated area. Should contact with the eyes occur, rinse the affected area with water for 15 minutes, and seek medical attention while rinsing is occurring.

When the latex solution sets, it forms rubber which can act as a glue or binding agent. Avoid getting the latex solution in eyes, hair, or fabric. There is no easy and safe way to remove latex once it is set into the rubber form. Old clothes, aprons, or smocks (borrowed from an art teacher) should be worn when using the latex solution. Clean the spoon or stirring stick by rinsing it with water before the latex has set. If spilled on a linoleum floor or Formica tabletop, rub the latex into a ball and wipe it up before it sets.

Unused latex can be stored in a closed container for future use. Cups covered with a film of liquid latex can be discarded in the trash.

Getting Ready

Pour vinegar to a depth of about 5 cm (2 in) in a labeled cup. Similarly pour liquid latex to a depth of about 5 cm (2 in) into a separately labeled cup. If you want to make colored rubber bands, add liquid tempera paint until a desired pastel shade is achieved and mix well with a stir stick.

Opening Strategy

Pour a small amount of latex into the palm of your hand. Taking care not to spill the latex on your clothes, rub the latex around your palm with a finger. Observe the latex congeal into a ball. Challenge the students to explain how this happens. (The heat of your hand causes the ammonia stabilizer to evaporate. With the ammonia gone, the latex congeals.) It may be easier to demonstrate the procedure before allowing the students to begin. Explain that in the activity, the vinegar neutralizes the ammonia in the latex suspension, allowing the latex to congeal.

Procedure

 Be careful during Steps 1 and 2 that the latex and vinegar do not splatter into your eyes, hair, or clothes. Be sure to wear goggles throughout this activity.

1. Dip your index finger up to the first joint in the vinegar. Remove your finger from the vinegar and hold it over the cup for about 10 seconds to allow the excess to drip into the cup.

2. Dip the same index finger up to the first joint in the liquid latex. Remove your finger from the latex and hold it over the cup for about 10 seconds to allow the excess to drip into the cup.

3. Dip the latex-coated finger back into the cup of vinegar and hold it there for 3–4 seconds. Remove your finger from the vinegar and allow the excess to drip into the cup for about 10 seconds.

4. With the point of a pencil, poke a small hole in the latex at the tip of your finger, and quickly and evenly roll the latex down your finger toward your hand.

5. Slide the "rubber band" off your finger. Set it aside for a few minutes while you make two or three more rubber bands.

6. Pull on the rubber bands to test their strength and stretchiness. Be careful not to pull too hard. Compare your rubber bands to those made by others in your group.

7. Wash your hands with soap and water to rinse off any remaining vinegar.

Variations

- Especially with younger children, you may prefer to make a rubber ball by pouring about 1 Tbsp latex into the bottom of a paper cup. Add 1 Tbsp vinegar and work the liquid back and forth with a stirring stick for a few minutes, then take the mixture out and form it into a ball. Compare the latex ball to a super ball made from sodium silicate and ethyl or isopropyl alcohol (See Activity 16, Making a Super Ball) as to their relative bounce and stability.

- To make larger rubber bands, dip the bottom of a plastic bottle or cup (e.g., dishwashing liquid bottle or hydrogen peroxide bottle) into a container with at least a 2-cm (1-in) depth of latex and then into a container with twice as much vinegar. (See Figure 1.) Try many different shapes and sizes of bottles to make the rubber bands. Once the larger rubber bands are made, compare commercially made rubber bands of similar size to the homemade ones.

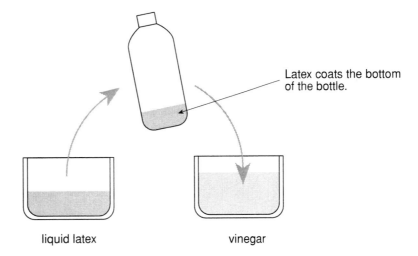

Figure 1: Dip the plastic bottle into liquid latex and then into vinegar.

- Have students set up their own company which manufactures rubber bands, latex-coated products, or products that have a rubber band as a component. Students should focus on the production, marketing, and sales of their product.

/>
Discussion

- Discuss the role that ammonia plays in the latex.
  Latex is a suspension of small globules of latex polymer in an ammonia solution. The ammonia keeps the latex globules apart from each other. When the vinegar is added, the ammonia is neutralized, and the latex globules stick together (congeal).

- Ask students to explain the observed differences between the homemade rubber bands and the commercial ones.
  The commercial bands are more uniform in thickness.

- Discuss other uses for latex besides rubber bands.
  Latex can be used for paint, erasers, balls, squeaky toys, gloves, tires, etc.

Explanation

Latex is the sap of the rubber tree, *Hevea brasiliensis*, which was originally found in the Amazon valley but is now cultivated in tropical areas around the world. To harvest the sap, a synthetic plant hormone, chlorethylpropionic acid, is used to stimulate the flow. The harvesters collect the sap in the early morning when the flow is greatest.

Liquid latex is made up of very small globules containing rubber-like molecules (called polyisoprene) suspended in a watery liquid. This suspension is an emulsion of rubber latex in water. Upon exposure to air, latex hardens into an elastic mass. In nature the gelled latex forms a type of plug that keeps the rubber tree from losing sap if the trunk is punctured. Trees can protect themselves from damage in this manner. A dilute aqueous solution of ammonia is added to latex taken from trees for commercial purposes to keep the latex from hardening. In this activity, vinegar is added to neutralize the ammonia, thus allowing the latex molecules to gel. Neutralization is a common acid-base reaction. The actual reaction occurs between the aqueous ammonia and the acetic acid present.

The individual rubber-like molecules in the latex suspension are giant macromolecules called polyisoprene. They have molecular weights ranging from 100,000 to several million. Polyisoprene is a type of polymer (poly=many; mer=unit); it is made of repeating (C_5H_8) units. (See Figure 2.) The shock absorbency of latex results from the fact that in the unstretched rubber the polymer chains fold back on each other like an accordion. Stretching the rubber straightens the folds in the chains; when released the chains return to their folded positions.

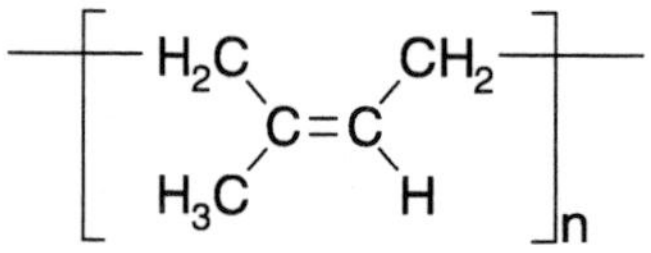

Figure 2: The repeating polyisoprene monomer that makes up the latex polymer

Key Science Concepts

- acid/base neutralization
- elasticity
- natural products
- polymers and their properties

Cross-Curricular Integration

Mathematics
Have students measure the distance that the rubber band travels when stretched and released. (Be sure the rubber bands are not aimed toward anyone when they are released.)

Social Studies
Relate the fact that latex rubber is grown in tropical regions of South America and shipped to the United States to the need for trade agreements with countries in these regions.

References

Jester, L.L. "A Chain Reaction," *Science and Children*. 1992, 29(4), 12–15.

Sarquis, A.M. "A Polymer Primer," *Science and Children*. 1992, 29(4), 14.

Painting with Elastomers

12

Is there art in chemistry or chemistry in art? This activity allows you to design and paint a T-shirt using polymers. Be creative and have fun!

Recommended Grade Level 2–12
Group Size .... individual
Time for Preparation .... 15–20 minutes
Time for Procedure .... Day 1: 30–45 minutes
                                                                          Day 2: 10–15 minutes (optional)

Materials

Procedure
Per Student
- 1 of the following articles to be painted:
  ○ T-shirt
  ○ shorts or pants
  ○ sweatshirt
  ○ hat
  ○ scarf
  ○ cloth shoes
  ○ swatch of fabric
- paper bag or waxed paper
- goggles

Per Class
- liquid latex (natural rubber)
- liquid tempera paints
- containers for the paints:
  ○ baby food jars
  ○ plastic margarine containers
  ○ plastic cups with lids
- paint brushes, stirring sticks, or cotton swabs
- old towels or paper towels
- soapy water for rinsing brushes
- (optional) vinegar, in several spray bottles
- (optional) black permanent markers
- (optional) dish pan for rinsing articles
- (optional) stencils purchased or made as described in Getting Ready

Extension
- milkweed or dandelion stems

Resources

Liquid latex can be purchased from a chemical supply company such as Flinn Scientific, P.O. Box 219, Batavia, IL 60510-0219, 800/452-1261.

• liquid latex—catalog # L0004 for 500 mL

Tempera paints and latex (under the name Pliatex Mold Rubber) can be purchased at an art supply store.

Safety and Disposal

Goggles should be worn when performing this activity. Liquid latex contains ammonia as a stabilizer. Ammonia or its vapors can damage the eyes. Contact lenses should not be worn when working with ammonia-containing products as gaseous vapors of ammonia can condense on the contact lens and cause damage to the eye. Use ammonia in a well-ventilated area. Should contact with the eyes occur, rinse the affected area with water for 15 minutes and seek medical attention while the rinsing is occurring.

When the latex solutions sets, it forms rubber which can act as a glue or binding agent. Avoid getting the latex solution in eyes, hair, or fabric. There is no easy and safe way to remove latex once it is set into the rubber form. Old clothes, aprons, or smocks (borrowed from an art teacher) should be worn when using the latex solution. Clean the spoon or stirring stick by rinsing it with water before the latex has set. If spilled on a linoleum floor or Formica tabletop, rub the latex into a ball and wipe it up before it sets.

The latex may be stored in tightly closed containers for future use. Paint brushes can be cleaned in soapy water. If latex paint is allowed to dry in the brush, the brush may be ruined.

Getting Ready

Prepare the paints by filling containers (e.g., baby food jars, plastic margarine dishes, plastic cups) half-full of liquid latex. Add liquid tempera paint until a pastel shade is achieved. Mix well. The colors of the paints will intensify with setting.

If desired, make or purchase stencils for the students to use. An example of a pattern for a stencil that you could use is shown in Figure 1.

Opening Strategy

Introduce the concept of polymers to the class by explaining the terms monomer (a molecule of a single unit) and polymer (a large molecule of repeating identical or similar subunits). These two terms may be illustrated using pop beads purchased from a toy store or gumdrops joined by toothpicks. Prepare a list of polymer products that come to mind, and have the students indicate those that they have come in contact with during the past three days.

SCIENCE IS FUN

Figure 1: A Science is Fun! logo to be used as a stencil for T-shirts

Procedure

1. Place a paper bag or waxed paper under the material to be decorated in case the paint bleeds.

2. (optional) If using stencils, trace the pattern onto the cloth. Any original designs can be traced or applied freehand if desired.

Be careful during Step 3 that the latex does not splatter into your eyes, hair, or clothes. Goggles must be worn throughout this activity.

3. Paint lightly and gently "scrub" the paint into the cloth with the brush. The colors become darker upon drying.
 Rinse the paint brushes in soapy water immediately after use.

4. Once painting is complete, either let the material air-dry or spray all painted areas with vinegar.

5. If vinegar is used, rinse the sprayed area with water by dipping it into a pan of water. Press the cloth between layers of a towel or paper towels to remove excess water. DO NOT WRING! Lay flat to dry overnight.

6. (optional) Once the cloth is completely dry, outline your design with black permanent marker.

Extension

- If milkweed plants or dandelion stems are available, compare their milky extract and its reaction with vinegar to the latex used and product formed in this activity.

Discussion

- Discuss why the painting should be air-dried instead of dried in a dryer.
  Excessive heat, like that in a dryer, causes the latex to become sticky, discolors the paint, and even begins to decompose the latex.

- In Step 4, the painting could be set into the fabric either by air-drying or by treating with vinegar. Discuss why either is an acceptable option.
  Latex is a suspension of small latex globules in an ammonia solution. For the latex to congeal, the ammonia has to be removed. This can be accomplished either by allowing the ammonia to evaporate overnight or by neutralizing it with the vinegar.

Explanation

As in Activity 11, "Making Rubber Bands," vinegar is added in this activity to neutralize the suspended latex (or the latex is air-dried to allow the ammonia to vaporize), thus allowing the latex molecules to congeal after they have penetrated the fabric. The congealed latex then sets into the fabric, creating the water-resistant, raised decorations. Tempera paint is added to provide color. See the Activity 11 Explanation for a more detailed discussion of latex.

Key Science Concepts

- acid/base neutralization
- natural products
- polymers and their properties
- suspensions

Cross-Curricular Integration

Language Arts
Have students write stories about how life would change if rubber was no longer available (e.g., What would cars or tennis shoes be like?).

Mathematics
Have students calculate the costs of making the painted T-shirts. Also, have them calculate how much they would have to charge for the painted T-shirts to make a profit of 10–20%.

Social Studies
Discuss Charles Goodyear's contributions to the rubber industry.

Have students research the history of rubber, the role of rubber in the economy of a country such as Brazil or Malaysia, or the relationship of latex production to rain forest deforestation.

Relate the use of "natural" and synthetic polymers in different products to the reason the world uses so many synthetic polymers.

References

Jester, L.L. "A Chain Reaction," *Science and Children.* 1992, 29(4), 12–15.

Sarquis, A.M. "A Polymer Primer," *Science and Children.* 1992, 29(4), 14.

Making Erasers

Scientists and engineers often face problems that involve developing a polymer-based product with specific properties and capabilities. This activity challenges students to prepare an eraser from latex and to use problem-solving strategies to determine which additives can be incorporated into the latex to yield the eraser with the best properties.

Recommended Grade Level 4–12
Group Size .... 1–4 students
Time for Preparation .... 15 minutes
Time for Procedure .... 60–75 minutes (+ 2–3 hours for the erasers to cure)

Materials

Procedure, Part 1
Per Group
- 2 3–5-oz paper or plastic cups
- 15 mL (1 Tbsp) liquid latex
- 15 mL (1 Tbsp) water
- 15 mL (1 Tbsp) vinegar
- 12-oz plastic cup or wash basin
- stirring stick or plastic spoon
- 1 of the following measuring devices:
  - tablespoon
  - 25- or 50-mL graduated cylinder
- paper towels
- marker for labelling cups
- goggles

Procedure, Part 2
Per Group
- 2 3–5-oz paper or plastic cups
- measuring spoon (½ tsp)
- 15 mL (1 Tbsp) liquid latex
- 15 mL (1 Tbsp) water
- 15 mL (1 Tbsp) vinegar
- sheet of white paper or index card
- (optional) food color or tempera paint

Per Class
- several abrasive substances, such as:
  - sand
  - flour
  - ground pumice
  - talc

○ table salt (sodium chloride, NaCl)
○ sawdust
○ ground cereal
○ corn starch
○ baking soda

Variation

- milkweed or dandelion stems

Resources

Liquid latex can be purchased from a chemical supply company such as Flinn Scientific Inc., P.O. Box 219, Batavia, IL 60510-0219, 800/452-1261.

- liquid latex—catalog # L0004 for 500 mL

Latex can also be purchased at an art supply store as Pliatex Mold Rubber.

Safety and Disposal

Goggles should be worn when performing this activity. Liquid latex contains ammonia as a stabilizer. Ammonia or its vapors can damage the eyes. Contact lenses should not be worn when working with ammonia-containing products as gaseous vapors of ammonia can condense on the contact lens and cause damage to the eye. Use ammonia in a well-ventilated area. Should contact with the eyes occur, rinse the affected area with water for 15 minutes and seek medical attention while rinsing is occurring.

When the latex solution sets, it forms rubber which can act as a glue or binding agent. Avoid getting the latex solution in eyes, hair, or fabric. There is no easy and safe way to remove latex once it is set into the rubber form. Old clothes, aprons, or smocks (borrowed from an art teacher) should be worn when using the latex solution. Clean the spoon or stirring stick by rinsing it with water before the latex has set. If spilled on a linoleum floor or formica tabletop, rub the latex into a ball and wipe it up before it sets.

Unused latex can be stored in a closed container for future use. Cups covered with a film of liquid latex can be discarded in the trash.

Getting Ready

For Part 1, pour about 15 mL (1 Tbsp) liquid latex and 15 mL (1 Tbsp) water into one labeled cup for each group. Pour about 15 mL (1 Tbsp) vinegar into a separate labeled cup for each group.

For Part 2, students will need more latex, water, and vinegar, but you should not pour out the latex more than about 5–10 minutes ahead of time as it will begin to congeal.

Opening Strategy

Ask students if they know how an eraser is made. Ask them if they know the difference between various types of erasers. Tell them they are going to make several erasers and determine which works best.

Procedure

Part 1: Make an Eraser

 During Steps 1 and 2 be careful that the latex does not spatter into your eyes, hair, or clothes. Goggles must be worn throughout this activity.

1. While stirring with a stick or spoon, slowly add the latex-water mixture to the vinegar. It is easiest if one person stirs the mixture while another person pours the latex-water mixture.

2. Using the stick or spoon, immediately remove the latex lump and rinse it in a large cup or a basin of water. The liquid remaining from the original mixture can be discarded down the drain. If using a cup, punch the latex into the bottom of a cup about half-full of water for a flat shape. This safely removes bubbles. If using a basin, squeeze and shape the lump into a ball or bar under the water.

 Beware of "bubbles" of latex. During squeezing, don't allow liquid latex in a bubble to splatter onto your clothes.

3. Squeeze out excess water from the ball of latex. Using paper towels, squeeze even more excess water from the latex lump.

4. Allow the ball of latex (your eraser) to dry on a towel for at least 2–3 hours.

5. Examine your eraser. Compare its properties to a commercial eraser. Consider the eraser's stretchiness, retention of shape after being stretched or smashed, ability to erase pencil and ink marks, and the condition of the paper after erasing.

Part 2: The Eraser Challenge

 Each group will need an additional 15 mL (1 Tbsp) of latex, water, and vinegar to perform this part of the activity. (See Getting Ready.) Each group should use a different abrasive material so that all are tested.

1. Sprinkle about ½ teaspoon of one of the abrasive materials into the latex-water mixture.

2. (optional) Add one drop of food color or tempera paint to the latex-water mixture to give the eraser color and to differentiate one group's product from another.

3. Repeat Part 1, Steps 1–5. (If using sand as the abrasive, make sure to thoroughly mix the sand and latex and spoon the sand/latex mixture from the bottom of the cup into the vinegar.)

4. Design a quantitative test to determine the erasing ability of the eraser. Vote to select one test for the entire class to use. For example, determine the number of times the eraser must pass over a mark made with a #2 pencil in order to erase the mark completely.

5. Perform the test and record the results. Compare the homemade erasers with commercial erasers, or enlist students from other classes to conduct user tests of the erasers to determine the preferred additive and eraser color.

6. Repeat the preparation using the best two eraser formulations to determine reproducibility of results.

Variation

- Have students gather milkweed or dandelion juice. These fluids, found in the stems of the plants, contain natural rubber and will congeal in the same way as latex. Have students rub some back and forth on their fingers to make it congeal.

Discussion

- Discuss the results from the comparison of the homemade erasers to commercial erasers in their ability to erase pencil marks.
  The homemade erasers should erase pencil marks as well as commercial erasers do.

- Ask the students to determine which additive improved the ability of the homemade eraser to erase pencil marks and to explain why.
  While some additives work better than others, any abrasive will increase the eraser's ability to erase by helping to physically scrape the pencil marks from the page. This process is similar to the way in which sandpaper removes paint from a wooden surface.

Explanation

As in Activities 11 and 12, "Making Rubber Bands" and "Painting with Elastomers," vinegar is added in this activity to neutralize the ammonia that holds the latex in suspension. In this activity, you see how a specific polymer has become functional because of its properties. The name "rubber" was given to congealed latex because of its early use in rubbing out pencil marks. Over the years, scientists and engineers have found ways to improve upon the existing polymer and give it additional desired properties as needed. Modern erasers contain a mixture of latex and vegetable oil. Pumice is added to ink erasers for a more abrasive quality.

Key Science Concepts

- acid/base neutralization
- chemical changes
- polymers and their properties
- product development

Cross-Curricular Integration

Art
Find out how latex is used in making professional props. Have students act as a makeup or props crew to design scars made of latex.

Home, Safety, and Career
Discuss the differences in cost between the homemade eraser and the commercial eraser. Advertising, packaging, and personnel costs should be addressed.

Language Arts
Have students write about their research or experimental findings, or have them write an advertising campaign and produce commercials for their products.

Life Science

Since the rubber tree is found in the Amazon valley, address the issue of rain forest devastation in relation to rubber production.

Mathematics

Have students develop a histogram or other graph of the results of the quantitative test performed in Part 2, Step 5, as a method of comparing and contrasting the performance of the homemade erasers to the commercial ones or the performance of the homemade erasers made with different abrasive materials.

Social Studies

Have students research the history of rubber or the role of rubber in the economy of a country such as Brazil or Malaysia.

Relate the issue of foreign relations and trade to the availability of the raw latex.

References

Berg, L., Eastern Green County Elementary School, Bloomfield, IN, personal communication.

Sarquis, A.M. "A Polymer Primer," *Science and Children.* 1992, 29(4), 14.

Glue Polymer

14

Turn common glue into gooey fun. Two recipes are included. Try them and find your favorite.

Recommended Grade Level 1–12
Group Size .... 1–4 students
Time for Preparation .... 20–30 minutes
Time for Procedure .... 15–20 minutes per part

Materials

Procedure, Parts 1–3
Per Group

You will need all of these materials for each part and for each additive in Part 3. You will need a new cup and bag for each part and additive.

- 5-oz paper cup
- stirring stick
- graduated cylinder or measuring spoons
- zipper-type plastic bag for storage (sandwich-size or bigger)
- goggles

Procedure, Part 1
Per Group
- 30 mL (2 Tbsp) white glue (Elmer's® glue works best.)
- 15 mL (1 Tbsp) Purex® Sta-flo liquid starch
- (optional) food color

Procedure, Part 2
Per Group
- (optional) food color

Per Class
- 1-L beaker or similar-sized container
- 400-mL or 600-mL beaker or similar-sized container
- 50/50 white glue/water mixture
- 4% borax solution (sodium tetraborate, $Na_2B_4O_7$) made from the following:
  ○ laundry borax (sodium tetraborate decahydrate, $Na_2B_4O_7 \bullet 10H_2O$)
  ○ water

Procedure, Part 3
Per Group
Additive 1
- 1½ sticks chalk, crushed (about 1 Tbsp) or 14 g (about 1 Tbsp) plaster of Paris (calcium sulfate hemihydrate, $CaSO_4 \bullet ½H_2O$)

Do not use anti-dust chalk.

- 30 mL (2 Tbsp) white glue
- 15 mL (1 Tbsp) Purex® Sta-Flo starch
- paper towel

Additive 2
- 5 mL (1 tsp) talcum powder
- 50/50 white glue/water mixture
- 5 mL (1 tsp) 4% borax solution

Additive 3
- 5 mL (1 tsp) talcum powder
- 10 mL (2 tsp) oil-free moisturizing lotion such as Revlon® Clean and Clear®
- 50/50 white glue/water mixture
- 5 mL (1 tsp) 4% borax solution
- (optional) food color

Procedure, Part 4
Per Group
- 10 drops vinegar
- 10 drops ammonia
- 2 disposable plastic pipets or droppers
- Petri dish or small beaker
- stirring stick
- water-soluble, felt-tip marker
- index card or plastic bag
- goggles

Extension
- egg white
- 3 paper envelope patterns
- 6 craft sticks
- flour
- white glue

Resources

White glue, laundry borax, vinegar, household ammonia, liquid starch, chalk, talcum powder, and oil-free moisturizing lotion can be purchased at a discount department store. Plaster of Paris can be purchased at a hardware store.

Safety and Disposal

Goggles should be worn when performing this activity. Household ammonia or its vapors can damage the eyes. It is recommended that contact lenses not be worn when working with ammonia as gaseous vapors may condense on the contact lens and cause damage to the eye. Use ammonia only in a well-ventilated area. Should contact with the eyes occur, rinse the affected area with water for 15 minutes. Medical attention should be sought while rinsing is occurring.

Some people have developed an allergic reaction to dry, powdered borax. As a result, care should be taken when handling it. Avoid inhalation and ingestion. Use adequate ventilation in preparing the borax solution and wash your hands after contact with the solid.

There is typically no danger in handling the Glue Putty, but students should wash their hands after use. Persons with especially sensitive skin or persons who know they are allergic to borax or detergent products should determine their sensitivity to the putty by touching a small amount. Should redness or itching occur, wash the area with a mild soap and avoid further contact.

Glue Putty does not readily stick to clothes, walls, desks, or carpet. However, students should be cautioned not to place it on wooden furniture, since it will leave a water mark. If the Glue Putty spills on the carpet, apply vinegar on the spot and follow with a soap-and-water rinse. Do not let the putty harden on the carpet. The Glue Putty will keep for a time if stored in a plastic bag. Discard the putty in a waste can when finished with it.

If you allow students to take the putty home, send the precautions and cleanup instructions from the preceding paragraph.

Getting Ready

 Some people have developed an allergic reaction to the powdered borax. Use caution when handling. See Safety and Disposal.

1. Prepare an approximately 4% sodium tetraborate solution for Parts 2 and 3 by dissolving 20 g (⅛ cup) borax (sodium tetraborate, $Na_2B_4O_7$) in 500 mL (1 pint) water.

2. Prepare a 50/50 white glue/water mixture for Parts 2 and 3 by mixing the white glue with an equal amount of water, allowing about 30 mL of the mixture per student. Stir thoroughly until well mixed.

3. For use by younger students, crush the chalk for Part 3 and place it in labeled plastic bags.

Opening Strategy

The nature of polymer chains can be shown through a simple kinesthetic activity as described in Kinesthetic Demonstrations and Simulations in Using the Activities in the Classroom.

Procedure

 If there is concern about the amount of materials needed for each group to perform all sections of this activity, you may choose to conduct one of the sections as a demonstration or assign different groups to each part and have the groups compare results.

Part 1: Starch/Glue Putty

1. Pour 30 mL (2 Tbsp) white glue into a paper cup.

2. (optional) Add 1–2 drops of food color to the glue. Mix thoroughly.

3. Add 15 mL (1 Tbsp) of starch while stirring. The polymer will begin to thicken on the stirring stick. Continue to stir and work the glue throughout.

4. Reach in and remove the putty with your fingers. Form it into a ball and rinse under running water.

5. Place the putty in a zipper-type plastic bag to prevent it from drying out.

Part 2: Borax/Glue Putty

1. Measure 30 mL (2 Tbsp) 50/50 glue/water mixture (prepared in Getting Ready) into the paper cup.

2. (optional) Add 1–2 drops of food color glue/water mixture. Mix thoroughly.

3. Stir in 10 mL (2 tsp) 4% borax solution (sodium tetraborate, $Na_2B_4O_7$). Stir continuously with the stirring stick until a mass of Glue Putty forms on the stirring stick.

4. Repeat Part 1, Steps 4 and 5.

Part 3: Additives for Putties

Additive 1: Chalk or Plaster of Paris

1. Pour the powdered chalk or plaster of Paris into the paper cup.

2. Add 15 mL (1 Tbsp) liquid starch to the powder and mix until all the powder is dispersed.

3. Add 30 mL (2 Tbsp) white glue to the mixture of starch and chalk or plaster of Paris.

4. Repeat Part 1, Steps 4 and 5.

Additive 2: Talcum Powder

1. Place 5 mL (1 tsp) talcum powder into a paper cup.

2. Add 45 mL (3 Tbsp) 50/50 white glue/water mixture.

3. (optional) Add 1–5 drops of food color to the glue solution. Mix well with a stirring stick.

4. Add 5 mL (1 tsp) 4% borax solution to the mixture. Stir continuously with the stirring stick until a mass of putty forms on the stick.

5. Reach in and remove the putty with your fingers. Pull any solid from the stirring stick. The putty may be sticky at first but will become less sticky with handling.

6. If the putty begins to dry, use a stirring stick to mix it with a small amount of water before storing it in a zipper-type plastic bag.

Additive 3: Talcum Powder and Moisturizing Lotion

1. Place 5 mL (1 tsp) talcum powder into a paper cup.

2. Add 10 mL (2 tsp) oil-free moisturizing lotion and 20 mL (4 tsp) 50/50 white glue/water mixture to the paper cup.

3. (optional) Add 1–5 drops of food color to the glue solution. Mix thoroughly.

4. Add 5 mL (1 tsp) of 4% sodium tetraborate solution into the paper cup. Stir continuously with the stirring stick until a mass of putty forms on the stick.

5. Remove the putty from the cup with your fingers. The putty may be sticky at first but will become less sticky with handling.

6. If the putty begins to dry, mix a small amount of oil-free moisturizer or water with the putty and place it in a zipper-type plastic bag for storage.

Part 4: Experimenting with the Putties

1. Experiment with each of the putties by squeezing it; by forming it into a ball and throwing it on a tile or linoleum floor; by pulling it gently and then quickly; and by pressing the putty on top of your name written with a water-soluble, felt-tip marker on the index card or plastic bag. Record your observations.

2. Compare putties with and without additives according to the procedures in Step 1 (e.g., stretchability, rigidity, texture, bounce).

3. Let some of each Glue Putty dry out for several days. Discuss the changes that have occurred. After each is dried out, try to get it to absorb some water.

4. De-gel and re-gel the putty:

➤ **This procedure should be performed as a teacher demonstration with younger students due to the use of the weak acid and base solutions. Older students can perform it as a hands-on activity.**

   a. Place a piece of putty about the size of a dime in a Petri dish or a small beaker. Add 5–10 drops of vinegar and stir with a stirring stick. Record any observations.

   b. Add 5–10 drops of household ammonia and stir well. Record any observations.

➤ **Do not allow the students to touch the re-gelled putty, as it may contain some ammonia which could damage their eyes or skin. Students can look at the putty and stir it with a stirring stick to make observations.**

Extension

Make two different glues and test them and commercial glue for their adhesive properties.

Egg White Glue: Separate the white of the egg from the yolk. Apply the egg white directly to the seal of an envelope pattern made from paper with no sealer and label it with "Egg White Glue" and the date. Seal the envelope. Also apply the egg white glue to two craft sticks and stick them together. Label and date the sticks.

Flour and Water Glue: Mix flour and water together to make a runny paste. Apply the flour glue to an envelope pattern and two craft sticks. Label each with "Flour and Water Glue" and the date.

Commercial Glue: Apply commercial glue to an envelope pattern and two craft sticks. Label each with "Commercial Glue" and the date.

Compare results. Continue checking each envelope and craft stick daily for changes in the adhesive properties of the homemade and commercial glues over a period of about two weeks. Discuss whether the homemade glues worked as well as the commercial glues.

Discussion

*   Ask students to compare the properties of the Glue Putty made with chalk (in Part 3) to the properties of the Glue Putty made in Part 1.
    The addition of the chalk caused the Glue Putty to be much drier, to be less stretchy and bouncy, and to have a much grittier texture.

- Ask students to compare the properties of the Glue Putty with added talcum powder and the properties of the Glue Putty with talcum powder/moisturizer (in Part 3) to the putty made in Part 2.
  The addition of the talcum powder caused the Glue Putty to be drier and more stretchy, and the addition of the talcum powder and moisturizer caused the Glue Putty to be smooth and more stretchy, but less bouncy.

- Explain how the vinegar and ammonia degelled and regelled the putty in Part 4.
  The starch contains borax. It is the borax that serves as a crosslinker between the polyvinyl acetate molecules found in the white glue. This crosslinking results in a jelly-like putty. When vinegar is added to the putty, the crosslinks are broken and the gel liquefies; the addition of ammonia neutralizes the vinegar and the gel returns.

Explanation

The Glue Putties made in Parts 1 and 2 are very similar to the polymer "Slime" which is made with polyvinyl alcohol and borax solution. (See Activity 15, Homemade "Slimes.") The difference between the two polymers is that the Slime contains polyvinyl alcohol and the Glue Putty contains white glue which is composed of polyvinyl acetate, water, and other ingredients.

Polyvinyl acetate is a polymer with the structure shown in Figure 1.

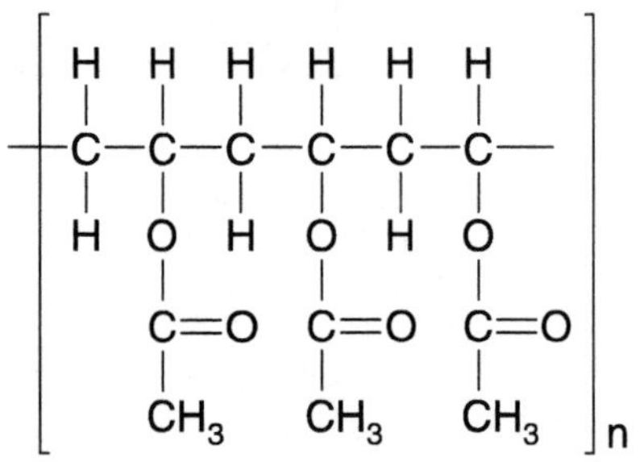

Figure 1: The structure of polyvinyl acetate

When starch, which contains borax, or borax is dissolved in water, some borate ($B(OH)_4^-$) ions form. These borate ions form crosslinks between polymer molecules. (See Figure 2.)

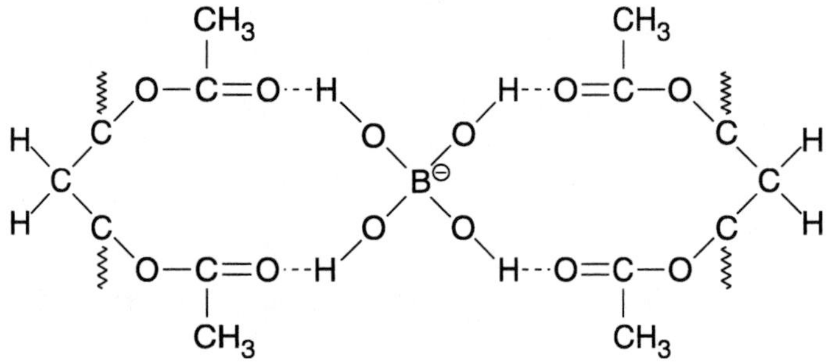

Figure 2: Possible hydrogen bonding sites on polyvinyl acetate

The crosslinks bond the different polymer chains together and change the properties of the polyvinyl acetate, making it more viscous (flows more slowly) and more bouncy.

In Part 3, the glue and starch both contain low-viscosity polymers. The addition of chalk, talcum powder, or plaster of Paris causes the formation of a semisolid compounded polymer with properties different than the three original components. The addition of the solids create additional crosslink sites and acts as a filler.

In Part 4, vinegar is added to a sample of the Glue Putty. The acid attracts the hydroxy (–OH) groups of the borate ion and thus draws the borate ion away from the polyvinyl acetate. This effectively removes the crosslinks and allows the polymer to liquefy. When the ammonia is added to the sample, it neutralizes the vinegar, and the borate ions can once more crosslink the chains of polymer, forming the putty.

Key Science Concepts

- acid/base neutralization
- chemical and physical changes
- crosslinking
- polymers and their properties

Cross-Curricular Integration

Language Arts
Have students develop a marketing strategy to sell the Putty to the public. They would have to develop a name for their product, design a suitable container in which to sell it, and create an ad campaign to get people to buy it.

References

"Gluep;" *Fun With Chemistry: A Guidebook of K–12 Activities;* Sarquis, M., Sarquis, J., Eds.; Institute for Chemical Education: Madison, WI, 1993; Vol. 2, pp 81–88.

Katz, D.A. *Investigations in Chemistry;* 1991–1992.

Lipscomb, R. *Polymer Chemistry: A Teaching Package for Pre-College Teachers;* National Science Teachers Association: Washington, DC, 1989; pp 180–181.

Meisch, K., Webster High School, Webster, NY, personal communication.

Sherman, M. "Polymers Link Science and Fun," presented at a workshop funded in part by the Industrial Sponsors, American Chemical Society, Polymer Chemistry Division, August 1993.

Warren, C., Cincinnati Hills Christian Academy, Cincinnati, OH, personal communication.

Woodward, L. *Polymers All Around You;* Terrific Science: Middletown, OH, 1992.

Homemade "Slimes"

You and your students will enjoy making and experimenting with a gooey polymer similar to the Slime® sold in many toy stores. Recipes for two types of Slime are included—conduct a "Slime Olympics!"

Recommended Grade Level 1–12
Group Size .... 1–4 students
Time for Preparation .... 30–45 minutes
Time for Procedure .... 30–45 minutes

Materials

Procedure, Part 1
Per Group
- 0.75 g (¼ tsp) guar gum
- 30 mL 4% borax solution (sodium tetraborate, $Na_2B_4O_7$) made from the following:
  - laundry borax (sodium tetraborate decahydrate, $Na_2B_4O_7 \bullet 10H_2O$)
  - water
- measuring cup, graduated cylinder, or calibrated cup to measure 80 mL (See Getting Ready.)
- 10-oz paper cup
- plastic spoon or stirring stick
- zipper-type plastic bag
- (optional) food color
- (optional) Lysol® Deodorizing Cleaner

Procedure, Part 2
Per Group
- 3 mL 4% borax solution
- 30 mL 4% polyvinyl alcohol solution purchased or made as described in Getting Ready
- 10-oz paper cup
- stirring stick
- measuring spoons (1-Tbsp and ½-tsp)
- zipper-type plastic bag
- (optional) food color
- (optional) Lysol Deodorizing Cleaner

Procedure, Part 3
Per Class
- water-soluble, felt-tip marker
- piece of paper
- timing device with a second hand
- ring stand
- ring clamp
- wide-mouthed funnel (The cut-off top of a 2-L bottle works well.)

Variation for Part 2

Per Class

All of the materials listed for Part 2 plus the following:

- 8% polyvinyl alcohol solution instead of a 4% solution

Resources

Guar gum and polyvinyl alcohol (as a 4% solution or granular solid) can be purchased from a chemical supply company such as Flinn Scientific, P.O. Box 219, Batavia, IL 60510-0219, 800/452-1261.

- guar gum—catalog # G0039 for 100 g
- polyvinyl alcohol solid—catalog # P0153 for 100 g
- 4% polyvinyl alcohol solution—catalog # P0210 for 1 L

Safety and Disposal

Some people have developed an allergic reaction to dry, powdered borax. As a result, care should be taken when handling it. Avoid inhalation and ingestion. Use adequate ventilation in preparing the borax solution and wash your hands after contact with the solid.

There is typically no danger in handling the Slimes, but students should wash their hands after use. Persons with especially sensitive skin or persons who know they are allergic to borax or detergent products should determine their sensitivity to the Slimes by touching a small amount. Should redness or itching occur, wash the area with a mild soap and avoid further contact.

If Slime spills on the carpet, apply vinegar to the spot and follow with a soap-and-water rinse. Do not let the Slime harden on the carpet. Do not place the Slime on natural wood furniture; it will leave a water mark.

Store the Slimes in plastic bags. If students are allowed to take the Slimes home, send a copy of the precautions and cleanup instructions from the preceding paragraph. Discard Slime in a waste can or flush it down the drain with lots of water.

Getting Ready

If using a precalibrated paper cup, add 80 mL water to the paper cups and use a permanent marker to place a line at the 80-mL mark. Precalibrated cups can help students to measure the water quickly without the need for more standard measuring equipment.

Prepare an approximately 4% borax solution by mixing 40 g (⅓ cup) laundry borax (sodium tetraborate decahydrate, $Na_2B_4O_7 \cdot 10\,H_2O$) in 1 L (about 1 qt) water while stirring.

Some people have developed an allergic reaction to the powdered borax. Use caution when handling.

If the 4% polyvinyl alcohol solution is not purchased, then a solution of approximately equal concentration can be prepared for use in Part 2 using one of the following methods:

a. Dissolve 40 g (⅓ cup) of polyvinyl alcohol in 1 L water while stirring. Heat the mixture on a hot plate over moderately high heat stirring constantly. The solution will initially be quite milky in color, but will clear when the polyvinyl alcohol is completely dissolved. The process may take up to 30–45 minutes. Cool the solution before using. If a slimy or gooey layer appears on the top during cooling, simply skim it off and discard.

b. Dissolve 40 g (⅓ cup) of polyvinyl alcohol in 1 L water in a microwave-safe container. Stir the solution and place it into a full-size microwave. Heat the solution on HIGH for 8 minutes, stirring every 1–2 minutes. Do not attempt to make more than 1 L at a time.

Opening Strategy

The nature of polymer chains can be shown through a simple kinesthetic activity as described in Kinesthetic Demonstrations and Simulations in Using the Activities in the Classroom.

Procedure

 For younger students you may wish to prepare the Slimes as a demonstration.

Part 1: Guar Gum Slime

1. Pour about 80 mL (⅓ cup) warm tap water into a paper cup. Use a stirring stick or plastic spoon to stir 0.75 g (¼ tsp) guar gum into the water; continue to mix until the guar gum dissolves and observe.

2. (optional) Add 2–5 drops of food color. Mix thoroughly.

3. While stirring, add about 30 mL (2 Tbsp) 4% borax solution to the guar gum mixture and observe.

4. Once the mixture has gelled, remove the Slime from the cup and knead it in your hands. **It takes a few minutes for the gel to set.**

5. Place the Slime in a zipper-type plastic bag to prevent it from drying out. A few drops of Lysol can be added to the Slime to minimize the formation of mold and extend the lifetime of the Slime.

Part 2: Polyvinyl Alcohol Slime

1. Pour about 30 mL (2 Tbsp) 4% polyvinyl alcohol solution into a paper cup.

2. (optional) Add 2–3 drops of food color. Mix thoroughly.

3. Pour 3 mL (about ½ tsp) 4% borax solution into the cup of polyvinyl alcohol solution. Stir constantly while the borax solution is being added.

4. Once the gel has formed, remove it from the cup and knead it in your hands.

5. Place the Slime in a zipper-type plastic bag to prevent it from drying out. A few drops of Lysol can be added to the Slime to minimize the formation of mold and extend the lifetime of the Slime.

Part 3: Slime Olympics

1. Experiment with each of the Slimes by squeezing it; by forming it into a ball and throwing it onto a tile or linoleum floor; by pulling it gently and then quickly; and by pressing the putty on top of your name written with a water-soluble, felt-tip marker. Record your observations.

2. A race can be held between the two Slimes. Set up a ring stand, ring clamp, and wide-mouthed funnel as shown in Figure 1. Place one of the Slimes in the funnel and begin timing. Stop timing when all of the Slime is on the table. Repeat for the other Slime recipe. The Slime with the fastest time is the winner.

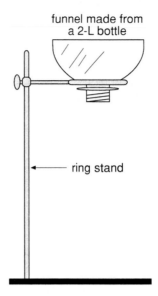

funnel made from
a 2-L bottle

ring stand

Figure 1: The apparatus for the Slime race

Variation

*   In Part 2, substitute an 8% polyvinyl alcohol solution for the 4% solution listed. The resulting Slime is less sticky and more viscous. To prepare the 8% polyvinyl alcohol solution, follow the directions in Getting Ready, but dissolve 80 g polyvinyl alcohol in 1 L water instead of 40 g. Stir the 8% polyvinyl alcohol solution overnight with a magnetic stirrer to remove any of the lumps of polyvinyl alcohol that may form.

Discussion

*   Discuss the differences between the Guar Gum Slime and the Polyvinyl Alcohol Slime.
    The Guar Gum Slime is less viscous (more runny) and can be stretched further before breaking than the Polyvinyl Alcohol Slime. Since the Guar Gum Slime is less viscous, it takes less time to flow through the funnel onto the table.

*   Ask students to describe the similarities between the Guar Gum Slime and the Polyvinyl Alcohol Slime.
    Both Slimes are clear and colorless (if food color is not added), can be molded into different shapes, will flow from a funnel over a period of time, will bounce (to a certain degree), and will become flat if left sitting on a flat surface.

*   Ask students to predict what would happen to a sample of each type of Slime if it were left sitting out for 2–3 days.
    Each sample of Slime would dry out as the water inside the gel evaporates. The dried-out Slimes are very stiff and brittle.

Explanation

A reversible crosslinked gel can be made from guar gum. Guar gum is a vegetable gum (molecular weight about 220,000) in which the water-soluble fraction (85%) has the structure shown in Figure 2. It is used as a protective colloid, stabilizer, thickener and film-forming agent for cheese, salad dressing, ice cream, and soups, and as a binding and disintegrating agent in tablet formulations, creams, and toothpaste.

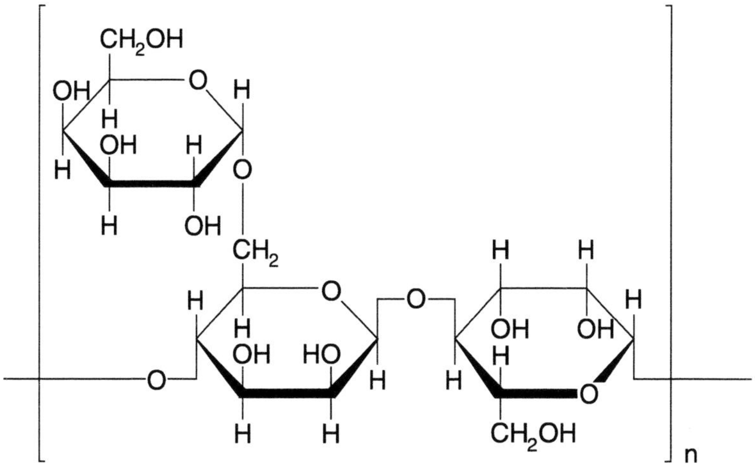

Figure 2: The water-soluble fraction of guar gum

The polyvinyl alcohol solution contains long polymer chains of polyvinyl alcohol that are dissolved in water. (See Figure 3.) Note that the alcohol groups (–OH) are on alternating carbons of the chain which may be several thousand carbon atoms long. The subscript n denotes a large number of multiples of this structure being repeated to form the long chain. Because these chains are very long, they interfere with each other's movement, causing the solution to be rather thick or viscous and to pour more slowly than water.

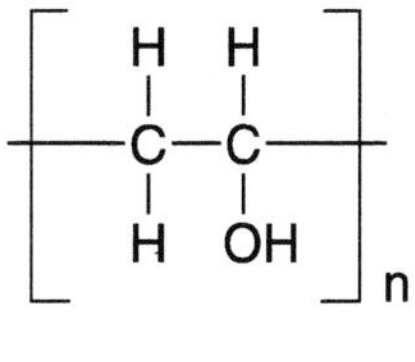

Figure 3: The structure of polyvinyl alcohol

Both Slime recipes are made by mixing the dissolved polymer with a solution of borax (sodium tetraborate, $Na_2B_4O_7$). When borax dissolves in water, borate ions ($B(OH)_4^-$) form. These borate ions can crosslink with the hydroxy (–OH) groups in either the guar gum or polyvinyl alcohol.

Two types of crosslinks are possible. (See Figures 4 and 5.) Figure 4 shows the reaction between the borate ion and the hydroxy (–OH) groups within the polymer structure.

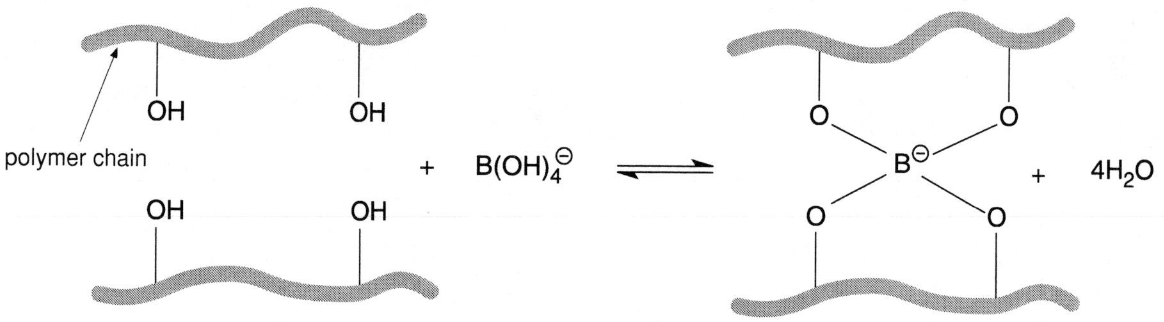

Figure 4: The reversible crosslinking of polyvinyl alcohol and the borate ion

Figure 5 shows the second type of crosslinking possible. While it is a weaker type of attraction than the covalent crosslinks resulting from the previous discussion (Figure 4), hydrogen bonding also plays a role in the gel's formation and properties.

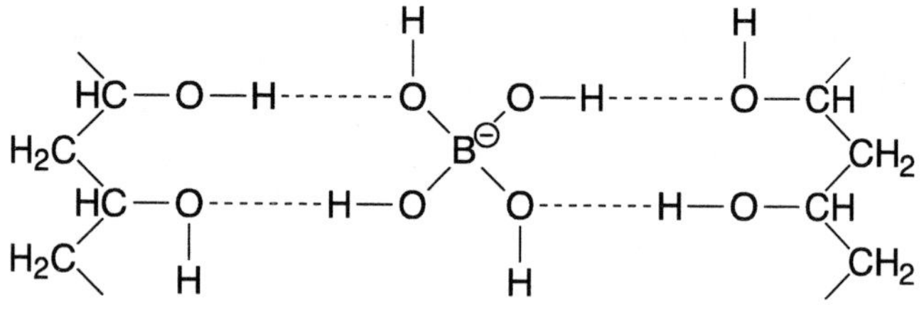

-------- = hydrogen bonds

Figure 5: Possible hydrogen bonding between polyvinyl alcohol and the borate ion

The crosslinking and bonding shown in Figures 4 and 5 result in a three-dimensional network of polymer chains connected by borate. Water molecules occupy most of the space within the three-dimensional network that comprises the gel.

"Slimes" belong to a class of materials that do not obey the usual laws of viscosity and are called non-Newtonian fluids. A low stress, such as slow pulling, allows Slimes to flow and stretch and even form a thin film. A high stress, such as pulling sharply, will cause Slime to break. Hitting a piece of Slime with a light hammer will not cause splashing or splattering, and the material will bounce to a small extent. If pushed through a tube, Slime will emerge with a swell (known as die swell in the plastics extrusion trade).

Key Science Concepts

- chemical reactions
- hydrogen bonding
- physical and chemical changes
- polymers and their properties

Cross Curricular Integration

Language Arts

For younger students, relate the Slime in the activity to the tar in the book *Watch Your Step, Mr. Rabbit!* by Richard Scarry (Random House, ISBN 0-679-81072-2). In this book, Mr. Rabbit gets stuck in tar. Relate the properties of Slimes to the properties of tar. Also read *The Slimy Book* by Babette Cole (ISBN 0-00-662840-0).

Have students write stories about waking up and discovering that the floor of the bedroom is covered in slime.

Have the students create and perform a commercial for selling Slime.

Have the students hypothesize how Slime would react in space.

Mathematics
Have the students calculate a cost analysis of their homemade Slimes versus some commercial brands.

References

Casassa, E.Z., et al. "The Gelation of Polyvinyl Alcohol with Borax," *Journal of Chemical Education.* 1986, 63, 57–59.

"Make-It-Yourself Slime;" *Fun With Chemistry: A Guidebook of K–12 Activities;* Sarquis, M., Sarquis, J., Eds.; Institute of Chemical Education: Madison, WI, 1993; Vol. 2, pp 67–75.

Sarquis, A.M. "Dramatization of Polymeric Bonding Using Slime," *Journal of Chemical Education.* 1986, 63, 60–61.

Sarquis, A.M., et al. *Science SHARE (Simple Hands-on Activities Reinforce Education);* Flinn Scientific: Batavia, IL, 1989; pp 43–48.

Selinger, B. *Chemistry in the Marketplace;* Harcourt Brace Jovanovich: Sydney, Australia, 1988.

Stroebel, G.G., et al. "Slime and Poly(Vinyl Alcohol) Fibers: An Improved Method," *Journal of Chemical Education.* 1993, 70(40), 893.

Woodward, L. *Polymers All Around You;* Terrific Science: Middletown, OH, 1992.

Making a Super Ball

How is a "super ball" made? What kind of "super material" is needed? The material used is a polymer, silicone, which gives the super ball its "super bounce."

Recommended Grade Level 7–12
Group Size .... individual
Time for Preparation .... 10–15 minutes
Time for Procedure .... 10–15 minutes

Materials

Opening Strategy
- modeling clay or Play-Doh®
- Ping-Pong™ ball
- Silly Putty®

Procedure
Per Student
- 2 tsp (10 mL) sodium silicate solution, $Na_2Si_3O_7$ (viscosity 40–42°Be.)
- ½ tsp (2.5 mL) 91–99% isopropyl alcohol
- small paper cup
- ½-tsp and 1-tsp measuring spoons or calibrated paper cup (See Getting Ready.)
- plastic gloves
- meterstick
- small plastic zipper-type bag
- (optional) food color
- goggles

Resources

Sodium silicate solution and plastic gloves can be purchased from a chemical supply company such as Flinn Scientific, P.O. Box 219, Batavia, IL 60510-0219, 800/452-1261.

- sodium silicate solution (40–42°Be.)—catalog # S0102 for 500 mL
- plastic gloves—catalog # AP3214 for 100 small gloves

Sodium silicate solution is sold in many hardware stores as water glass. Magic Rocks sold in toy stores for growing crystals contains a bag of sodium silicate solution which can also be used. Magic Rocks can also be mail-ordered from Craft House Corporation, 2101 Auburn Ave., Toledo, OH 43696. 91–99% isopropyl alcohol is available in pharmacies.

Safety and Disposal

Goggles should be worn when performing this activity. Sodium silicate solution is an irritant to the skin and harmful if swallowed. Avoid contact with the eyes and mucous membranes. In case of contact, flush the area well with water. If contact is made with the eyes, flush with water while seeking medical attention. Plastic gloves should be worn. All students should wash their hands after completing the activity.

Isopropyl alcohol is flammable. Avoid use around flames. All unused sodium silicate solutions and isopropyl alcohol solutions can be saved for future use.

The super balls are basic with a pH of about 10 and should always be handled while wearing goggles, plastic gloves, and old clothes. After completing the activity, the super balls should be discarded in the trash. Do not allow the students to take the super balls out of the classroom.

Getting Ready

Pour 10 mL water into a paper cup and use a permanent marker to mark a line at the water level. Mark a cup for each student at this level. This will enable students to measure the amount of sodium silicate solution needed without using graduated cylinders.

Opening Strategy

Compare bouncing characteristics of three balls: a ball of modeling clay or Play-Doh, a Ping-Pong ball, and a ball of Silly Putty. Drop the clay ball onto the floor or a desktop. It will produce little or no bounce, and should show significant deformation at the point of impact. Next try the Ping-Pong ball. It should bounce well, and because it is rigid, it will show no permanent deformation. Now drop the Silly Putty ball. It will bounce well, and like the Ping-Pong ball, it should not show any permanent deformation. However, it is also moldable like the clay. Ask the students to think about how a material can be both rigid and fluid, and ask them if they can think of any other materials that have this characteristic (e.g., Slime).

Procedure

1. While wearing plastic gloves, place 2 tsp (10 mL) sodium silicate solution ($Na_2Si_3O_7$) into a small paper cup. (This should be just enough to cover the bottom of the cup.)

2. (optional) Add 1–2 drops of food color to make a colored ball.

3. Measure out ½ tsp (2.5 mL) 91–99% isopropyl alcohol.

4. Speed is important in this step: Add the alcohol to the sodium silicate and stir with your gloved fingers for 3 seconds.

5. Pour the forming "solid" into the palm of one of your gloved hands. Gently press with the gloved fingers of your other hand until you form a ball.
 Pressing too hard will cause the ball to crumble.

6. While continuing to wear gloves, experiment with the super ball. Have a bouncing contest to see which ball has the highest bounce when dropped from 4 feet. Measure the height of the bounce and record your observations.

7. Store the ball in a small plastic zipper-type bag.

8. Wash your hands thoroughly after playing with the super ball.

9. Examine the ball after it has sat overnight in the closed bag.
➤ **To keep the ball round overnight, place the super ball in the end of one of the plastic glove fingers and tightly tie the finger shut. If left in a plastic bag, it will flatten and be very difficult to re-form into a ball.**

Extension

- This condensation polymerization process can be illustrated as described in Kinesthetic Demonstrations and Simulations in Using the Activities in the Classroom.

Discussion

- Ask students why it is important to wear plastic gloves and goggles while making and handling the super ball.
  The sodium silicate solution is extremely basic with a pH of about 10. Solutions at this pH can be a skin irritant and can damage the eyes.

- Ask students why the super ball can bounce so high.
  Silicone is a polymer which has a crosslinked structure. This crosslinked structure causes the polymer to exhibit non-Newtonian properties, one of which is becoming rigid when struck with a sharp blow. The impact energy is not absorbed in permanently deforming the ball (as it was with the clay in the Opening Strategy). Instead, much of it remains as mechanical energy and is used to make the ball bounce.

Explanation

Silicone, which is the polymer that makes up the super ball, is produced by a process called condensation polymerization. For silicone, the monomer units are the silicate ion and isopropyl alcohol. When sodium silicate ($Na_2Si_3O_7$) is mixed with isopropyl alcohol, the silicate units begin to link up with the isopropyl groups to form long polymer chains while releasing a water molecule. This polymerization reaction produces a rubber-like polymer, silicone. Unlike most organic polymers you may know (plastics, Slime, etc.), the silicone polymer does not have a backbone of carbon atoms. Its backbone is a repeating chain of silicon and oxygen atoms bonded together. (See Figure 1.)

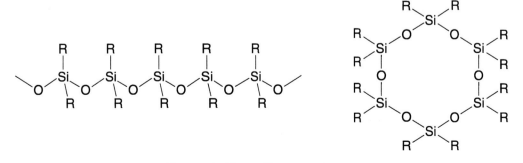

Figure 1: Two silicone polymers

Crosslinking can occur between the silicone chains through the sharing of an oxygen atom. (See Figure 2.) This crosslinking accounts for the super ball's "super" bounce.

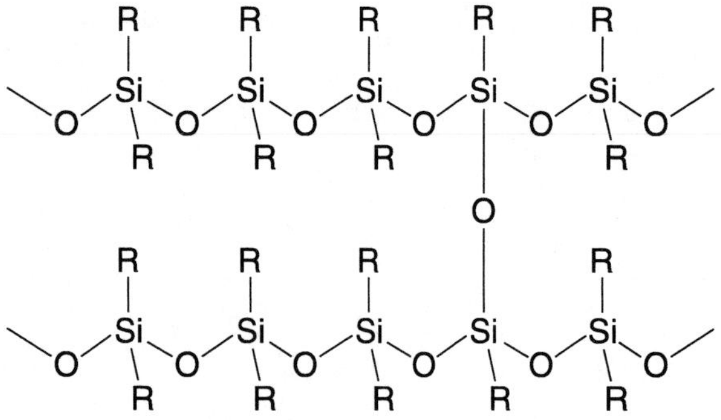

Figure 2: Crosslinking between two adjacent silicone polymer strands

The silicone polymer that is made in this activity is much like commercial Silly Putty. Both polymers are good examples of non-Newtonian fluids. This means that they can act like a fluid, but do not obey all of the same rules that many common fluids such as water do. For example, these polymers will flow (slowly) if left undisturbed. With gentle pressure they can be shaped like clay. Under intense pressure (like that caused by hitting the floor at high speed) they will become rigid. The impact energy is not absorbed in permanently deforming the ball (as it was with the clay in the Opening Strategy). Instead, much of it remains as mechanical energy and is used to make the ball bounce. It is this peculiar characteristic of some polymers that lets the silicone have some of the characteristics of both the clay ball and the Ping-Pong ball. Some organic polymers, such as Slime, also show characteristics of non-Newtonian fluids.

Key Science Concepts

- elastic and inelastic collisions
- inorganic polymers
- non-Newtonian fluids
- polymers and their properties

Cross-Curricular Integration

Language Arts
Our bodies are made mainly of carbon-based polymers. Have students write stories about "super beings" whose bodies are made of silicon-based polymers.

Suppose you were suddenly given "super" powers. Have the students write short stories about such experiences.

References

Borgford, C.L.; Summerlin, L.R. *Chemical Activities,* teacher ed.; American Chemical Society: Washington, D.C., 1988; pp 89–90.

Gillespie, R.J.; Humphreys, D.A.; Baird, N.C.; Robinson, E.A. *Chemistry;* Allyn and Bacon: Boston, 1989; pp 1003–1005.

A Water-Absorbent Polymer

How can baby diapers absorb so much liquid without leaking? Disposable diapers have a water-absorbent polymer in them called sodium polyacrylate. Sodium polyacrylate is a major ingredient not only in diapers, but also in some types of potting soil, water beds, and fuel filters for automobiles or jets. In this activity, students investigate the relationship between the amount of water absorbed by the polymer and the type of liquid added.

Recommended Grade Level 4–12
Group Size .... 1–4 students
Time for Preparation .... 20 minutes
Time for Procedure .... Part 1: 15 minutes
Part 2: 30–45 minutes

Materials

Opening Strategy
- warm tap water
- disposable diaper (any brand)
- measuring cup
- clear beaker or cup
- 2 tsp table salt (sodium chloride, NaCl)
- stirring stick

Procedure, Part 1
Per Class
- 3 identical, opaque containers
- 0.5 g (¼ tsp) sodium polyacrylate
- measuring spoons (¼ tsp and 1 Tbsp)
- measuring cup or 50-mL beaker

Procedure, Part 2
Per Group
- 2.5 g (1¼ tsp) sodium polyacrylate
- 5 tsp table salt
- 400-mL or 600-mL beaker, jar, or similar container
- stirring stick or plastic spoon
- calibrated cup or graduated cylinder
- measuring spoons (1 tsp and ¼ tsp)
- goggles

Per Class
- 4 1-L containers
- measuring spoons or balance (to prepare solutions)
- (optional) permanent marker

- 9 g (2 tsp) table salt
- 9 g (1½ tsp) potassium chloride (KCl)
- 9 g (1¼ tsp) sugar
- 4 L (1 gal) distilled water

➤ **Tap water can be substituted; results will not be as dramatic.**

Variations

Per Group
- 2 paper cups
- 1 g (¼ tsp) sodium polyacrylate
- 1.1 g (¼ tsp) table salt
- 1.8 g (¼ tsp) sugar

Per Class
- generic-brand disposable diapers
- name-brand disposable diapers
- 1 L 0.9% sodium chloride solution

Extension

- Magic Grow Dinosaurs
- some of the following liquids:
  ○ salt water
  ○ sugar water
  ○ alcohol
  ○ hot water
  ○ ice water
- access to a refrigerator

Resources

Sodium polyacrylate can be purchased from a chemical supply company such as Flinn Scientific, P.O. Box 219, Batavia, IL 60510-0219, 800/452-1261.

- potassium chloride, crystal—catalog # P0183 for 100 g
- sodium polyacrylate—catalog # W0013 for 100 g

Potassium chloride can also be purchased at a grocery as "lite salt" (Salt Sense). The Magic Grow Dinosaurs are sold in toy and novelty stores.

Safety and Disposal

Goggles should be worn when performing this activity. The sodium polyacrylate is non-toxic; however, the solid and dust can cause dryness and irritation of the mucous membranes (eyes, nose, mouth). Therefore, students should be told NOT to smell the powder. (It doesn't have any particular smell.)

Store the excess sodium polyacrylate in an airtight container for future use. Dispose of the gel in the trash where students cannot get to it. Alternatively, pour sodium chloride (NaCl) into the gel until it liquefies, stir well, and flush down the drain with plenty of water. Do not put the untreated gel down the sink, as it could clog the sink.

Getting Ready

Pour 50 mL water into a paper cup and use a permanent marker to mark a line at the water level. Mark a cup for each group at this level. This will enable students to measure the amount of water needed without using graduated cylinders.

Prepare a 0.9% (weight/volume) solution for each of the following solids by dissolving 9 g solid in 1 L distilled water: potassium chloride (KCl), table salt (sodium chloride, NaCl), and sugar.

For Part 1, place about 0.5 g (¼ tsp) sodium polyacrylate in one of three identical, opaque containers. Add about 15 mL (1 Tbsp) water to the sodium polyacrylate to create a gel that will not fall out of the container when tipped.

Opening Strategy

Pour cupfuls of warm water into a disposable baby diaper. Gently rocking the diaper back and forth to allow the water to be evenly distributed between additions, count the number of cups of water you can add before no more water is absorbed. Ask the students what is holding all of the water in the diaper. Open up this waterlogged diaper and scoop the gel out into a clear beaker or cup. Ask the students if they know of a way to get the gel to release the water. Sprinkle table salt (sodium chloride, NaCl) into the gel, stir with a stirring stick, and observe it as it liquefies.

Procedure

Part 1: Where Did The Water Go? (Teacher Demonstration)

1. Place the three identical containers in front of the class and pour about 50 mL water (about ¼ cup) into the container containing the gelled sodium polyacrylate.

2. Shuffle the three containers around and challenge the students to remember which container you placed the water in because you are going to dump the one that is chosen on the floor.

3. Have the students indicate the containers that DO NOT contain the water. Finally when they get to the one which they think contains the water, turn it over to show no water spillage.

4. Have the students speculate what happened.

Part 2: Experimenting with Sodium Polyacrylate

1. Add 0.5 g (¼ tsp) sodium polyacrylate to the 600-mL beaker or similar-sized container.

2. Add distilled water in 25–50 mL increments until the polymer can no longer absorb water. Record the total volume of water added.

3. Sprinkle 1 tsp table salt (sodium chloride, NaCl) onto the gel remaining in the container and stir with a stirring stick or plastic spoon. (This is the point when the container can be tipped and water flows freely.) Discard as described in Safety and Disposal. Thoroughly rinse and dry the container.

4. Repeat Steps 1, 2, and 3 substituting the following solutions for the distilled water used in Step 2: tap water; 0.9% sodium chloride solution (NaCl); 0.9% potassium chloride (KCl); and 0.9% sugar solution. Record the volume required for each solution and compare results with that for distilled water.

 The 0.9% sodium chloride solution represents the typical sodium chloride concentration in urine.

Discussion

- Discuss the relationship between the activity in Part 1 and the baby diaper used in the Opening Strategy.
  The baby diaper was able to hold so much water because of the polymer inside it (sodium polyacrylate) which absorbs all of the water. In Part 1, the water "magically" disappeared because one of the containers held some of the same polymer found in the baby diaper.

- Ask students to rank the solutions from greatest volume to smallest volume absorbed in Part 2.
  Distilled water, sugar water, tap water, 0.9% potassium chloride (KCl), and 0.9% sodium chloride (NaCl). See sample data.

- Discuss why the amount of tap water absorbed was smaller than the amount of distilled water absorbed.
  Tap water contains dissolved salts in the form of ions which do not allow the gel to form completely as distilled water does.

Variations

- Instead of adding solutions of salt and sugar in water, try using the solids. Sprinkle 0.5 g (¼ tsp) sodium polyacrylate into each of two cups. To the first cup, add 1.1 g (¼ tsp) table salt (sodium chloride, NaCl) and 50 mL of tap water. Stir well and observe. To the second cup, add 1.8 g (¼ tsp) sugar and 50 mL tap water. Stir well and observe. Challenge the students to develop an explanation for the difference between the actions of the salt and the sugar.

- Compare generic-brand disposable diapers to name brands with the 0.9% sodium chloride solution (simulated urine) to see if the more expensive name brand diapers hold more urine than the generic brand.

- Devise a test to determine the effect of hot and cold water on the gelling process.

Extension

- Experiment with Magic Grow Dinosaurs by putting them in salt water, sugar water, alcohol, hot water, or ice water to see how the different liquids change the rate of growth. Investigate the effect of temperature on the growth of the creatures by keeping some "critters" in a warm place and others in a refrigerator; compare the rate of growth. This activity has great possibilities for use in the science classroom for making observations, collecting data, graphing, making hypotheses, and drawing a conclusion.

Sample Data

Sodium Polyacrylate Sample	Kind of Liquid Added	Amount of Liquid Absorbed
0.5 g	distilled water	200 mL
0.5 g	tap water	120 mL
0.5 g	0.9% sodium chloride solution	35 mL
0.5 g	0.9% potassium chloride solution	40 mL
0.5 g	0.9% sugar solution	195 mL

Explanation

Most common synthetic polymers are "water-hating" (hydrophobic), which means that they do not absorb water. Hydrophobic polymers are used in products such as plastic cups, bags, and raincoats. Certain other polymers are "water-loving" (hydrophilic), which means that they absorb water. Many natural polymers such as cotton fibers are hydrophilic. One example of a synthetic hydrophilic polymer is sodium polyacrylate. It attracts water and swells as the water is absorbed.

Sodium polyacrylate contains negatively charged carboxylate groups and positively charged sodium ions. (See Figure 1.) While the polymer molecule is too large to actually dissolve in water, the charged groups on the polymer chain give it a very high affinity for water. The water molecules orient themselves around the negatively charged carboxylate groups. The water is drawn into the matrix of the polymers chains, forming a gel which can swell to several hundred times its original size. When the polymer swells, the distance between the charged carboxylate groups is increased (decreasing repulsive forces) and the sodium ions become hydrated (surrounded by water molecules) and distributed throughout the gel.

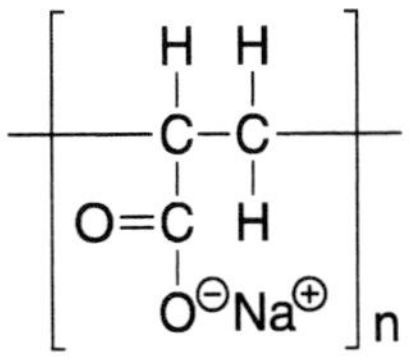

Figure 1: The structure of sodium polyacrylate polymer

The polymer does not swell as much in salt solutions because the ions from the salt interfere with the attractions between water and the carboxylate groups. Increasing the concentration of cations in the solution (e.g., by using 0.9% sodium chloride solution, which is the typical sodium chloride concentration in urine) increases the number of cations in close proximity to the carboxylate groups. The strong ionic attraction of the positive cations for the negative charge of the carboxylate groups decreases the number of water molecules that can be held in the gel of the polymer matrix. This is also the reason that sodium polyacrylate does not gel as well in tap water as it does in distilled water—tap water contains dissolved ions.

In contrast, molecular compounds (e.g., sugar, alcohol, etc.) or insoluble ionic compounds (e.g., calcium carbonate) do not seem to have an effect on the swelling of the polymer. This is due to the fact that the dissolved species (sugar molecules, etc.) have no charge and are not attracted to the carboxylate groups. Since there is no attraction, none of the water molecules are displaced and the gel remains intact.

Superabsorbent polymers are used in some brands of disposable diapers and in filtration units that remove moisture from automobile and airplane fuels. These polymers can also be incorporated into soil to help the soil retain water.

Key Science Concepts

- consumer products
- ionic attractions
- polymers and their properties

Cross-Curricular Integration

Earth Science
Discuss the impact of increasing polymer production from petroleum products on the world's supply of oil.

Discuss the environmental impact of disposable diapers versus cotton cloth diapers.

Life Science
Experiment with the superabsorber as part of the soil used for growing plants. Test the effect on the plants grown in soil containing the superabsorber and in soil without the superabsorber during drought conditions.

Mathematics
Have the students graph the results from the experiment.

References

Sherman, M. "Polymers Link Science and Fun," presentation at a workshop funded in part by the Industrial Sponsors, American Chemical Society, Polymer Chemistry Division, Washington, D.C., August 1993.

"Superabsorbent Polymer;" *Fun With Chemistry: A Guidebook of K–12 Activities;* Sarquis, M., Sarquis, J., Eds.; Institute of Chemical Education: Madison, WI, 1993; Vol. 2, pp 95–99.

Woodward, L. *Polymers All Around You;* Terrific Science: Middletown, OH, 1992.

Cellophane Tape Kaleidoscope 18

Students have fun making inexpensive kaleidoscopes while learning about the interaction of light with some types of polymers.

> **Recommended Grade Level** 3–12
> **Group Size** .... individual
> **Time for Preparation** .... 25 minutes
> **Time for Procedure** .... 60 minutes

Materials

Opening Strategy
- Polaroid® sunglasses
- overhead projector

Procedure, Part 1
Per Class
- half of a 7½-in x 7½-in polarizing film sheet
- 2 4.5-cm x 4.5-cm (about 1.8-in x 1.8-in) square pieces of polarizing film
- 1 sheet of black construction paper
- transparent tape
- overhead projector

Procedure, Part 2
Per Class
- 2 4.5-cm x 4.5-cm (about 1.8-in x 1.8-in) square pieces of polarizing film
- cellulose acetate sheet (clear overhead sheet)
- heat gun or hair dryer
- overhead projector
- various clear plastic items (e.g., plastic protractors, petri dishes, clear L'eggs® pantyhose eggs)
- corn syrup
- beaker

Procedure, Part 3
Per Student
- cardboard tube from a roll of toilet paper or paper towels
- 2 4.5-cm x 4.5-cm (about 1.8-in x 1.8-in) square pieces of polarizing film
- 5-oz paper cup
- inexpensive cellophane tape (The more expensive "magic" brands will not work.)
- black felt-tipped pen or marker
- scissors
- (optional) pieces of polystyrene "windows" from envelopes

Resources

The polarizing film sheets can be purchased from a science education supply company such as Edmund Scientific, 101 E. Gloucester Pike, Barrington, NJ 08007, 609/573-6250.

- polarizing film sheets—catalog # F37-350 for a square sheet (7.5 in x 7.5 in) which makes 16 squares of the desired size

Getting Ready

1. Ask the students to bring in toilet paper tubes or paper towel tubes from home.

2. For Part 1, make a polarizing-film circle overhead as follows:

   a. Cut 20 wedges (3-cm x 9-cm) from a polarizing film sheet as shown in Figure 1. Start by cutting the polarizing film sheet in half lengthwise and making marks every three centimeters along the long axis of the polarizing film sheet. Using these marks, cut out the wedges making sure that each wedge has two equal sides. By making the wedges have two equal sides, you should be able to get 11 wedges from half of a polarizing film sheet.

   b. Next, tape the wedges together to make a circle. Use transparent tape so the tape won't interfere with the light passing through the polarizing-film circle. As you tape the wedges together, try not to leave spaces between wedges and in the center of the circle. You may have to cut one of the last wedges smaller to complete the circle.

   c. In a piece of black construction paper, cut a hole with a diameter slightly smaller than the polarizing-film circle. Mount the circle in this frame of black construction paper to make it easier to use on the overhead.

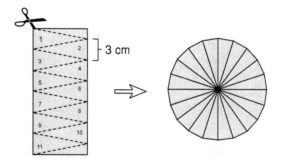

Figure 1: The polarizing-film wedges and the polarizing-film circle overhead

3. For Part 3, cut the polarizing film sheet into squares before the activity begins. Using a paper cutter, cut the large (7.5-in x 7.5-in) square sheets into 16 equal squares. Cut enough squares so that each student can have two pieces.

Opening Strategy

Show students a pair of Polaroid sunglasses. Ask students if they know how these sunglasses work. Explain that the lenses of the sunglasses are polarizers and have the ability to block out some of the sunlight. Demonstrate how the Polaroid lenses or polarizing film interacts with the light on the stage of the overhead projector.

Illustrate how light interacts with polarizing film by doing a kinesthetic demonstration. Ask for three volunteers and have two of the volunteers stand about three feet apart. These two represent the orientation of the polymer chains in the polarizing film on the stage of the overhead. Have the third volunteer (representing one plane in which light can travel) do a somersault between the two students. This shows how one plane of light from the overhead projector can pass through the polymer chains in the polarizing film. (See Figure 2a.) This represents the effect when the light is in the same plane as the polarizing paper.

Next, have the third volunteer roll like a log toward the other volunteers. He or she should be stopped by the legs of the two volunteers. This shows how other planes of light from the overhead projector are blocked by the polymer chains of the polarizing film sheet. (See Figure 2b.) This is the reason polarizing paper only allows one plane of light through it.

Figure 2: Kinesthetic demonstration of how light is affected by a polarizing film sheet

Procedure

Part 1: Polarizing-Film Circle
1. Tape one piece of polarizing film over the front glass on the head of an overhead projector.

2. Place a second piece of polarizing film directly on the stage of the projector.

3. Turn on the overhead projector and view the light on the screen as you slowly turn the polarizing film on the projector stage. Explain that the screen is bright when the polymer chains in both polarizing film sheets are oriented in the same direction (parallel) and the screen is dark when the polymer chains in the second polarizing film sheet are perpendicular to the ones in the first polarizing film sheet.

4. Show the students the polarizing-film circle overhead (prepared in Getting Ready), explain how it was made, and ask them to predict what will appear on the screen when you place it on the overhead.

5. Place the polarizing-film circle overhead on the stage of the overhead projector in place of the polarizing film sheet. Slowly turn the circle clockwise 360°. Observe the results.

Part 2: Various Plastics and Other Materials
1. Repeat Part 1, Steps 1–3, and then orient the polarizing film sheets so that no light will appear on the screen. Ask students to predict what will happen when you place a 30-cm x 1-cm piece of unstretched cellulose acetate (clear overhead sheets) on the stage of the overhead. Note the results.

2. Heat the piece of cellulose acetate using a heat gun and stretch it lengthwise.

3. Ask students to predict what will appear on the screen when you place the newly stretched sample on the stage again. Note the results.

4. Place different types of clear molded plastic objects (petri dishes, picnic-style knives, forks, and spoons, plastic protractors and stencils, clear L'eggs pantyhose eggs, polystyrene drinking glasses, etc.) on the stage of the overhead and note the results.

5. Tell students that plastics are not the only molecules that can rotate polarized light. Add corn syrup to a beaker, and set it on the stage of the overhead as was done with the plastic items. (A circular spot of colored light should appear on the screen. This is due to the fact that corn syrup solution contains sugar molecules (fructose) that rotate the light that passes through the first piece of polarizing film. Since the light has been rotated by the sugar molecules, the colored light has been rotated enough so that it can pass through the second piece of polarizing film and project onto the screen.)

Part 3: Making the Kaleidoscope

1. Place the end of a cardboard tube on one of the polarizing film pieces and trace around it with a felt-tipped pen or marker.

2. Cut out the polarizing-film circle and tape it to the end of the cardboard tube.

3. Cover the polarizing-film circle with many different-sized pieces of cellophane tape placed randomly onto the circle. (See Figure 3.)

➤ **Using more layers of tape placed over the polarizing-film circle produces better results.**

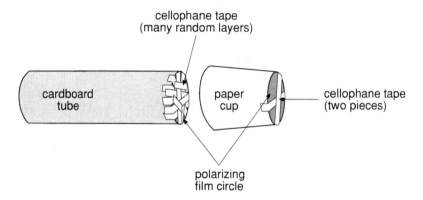

Figure 3: The kaleidoscope setup

4. (optional) Add curving areas to the design by cutting pieces of polystyrene windows from envelopes and taping them over the polarizing-film circle on the cardboard tube. These pieces of polystyrene replace the layers of tape that cover the end of tube.

5. Using scissors, cut out the bottom of a 5-oz paper cup. Place the cup, bottom-side down, on the second piece of polarizing film and trace around it with a felt-tipped pen or marker.

6. Cut out the polarizing-film circle and, using only two pieces of tape, tape the circle to the bottom of the paper cup. (See Figure 3.)

7. Place the cardboard tube inside the paper cup and look through the tube while holding the "kaleidoscope" up to the light. Rotate the paper cup and enjoy the colored light show.

Discussion

- Challenge the students to pictorially illustrate what plane polarized light is and how it differs from nonpolarized light.
  See Figure 4.

- Ask the students to explain what crossed polarizing film sheets are and how they would affect the transmittance of light.
  Crossed polarizing film sheets are two sheets of polarizing film that are oriented so that no light can pass through them. Light waves travel in all directions. However, if a polarizing film sheet is placed in the light's path, only the light in a single plane can pass through it. The plane of light can continue through a second polarizing film sheet if the polymer chains in the second polarizing film sheet are parallel to those in the first sheet. If the polymer chains in the second sheet are perpendicular to those in the first sheet, then the plane of light will be blocked.

Explanation

Light travels as waves just as sound does. The light from the sun or from a light bulb is a mixture of waves traveling in all directions. When a polarizer, such as a piece of polarizing film, is placed in the light's path, only light in a single plane can pass through the polarizer. (See Figure 4.) Light traveling in other planes is blocked and cannot pass through the polarizer.

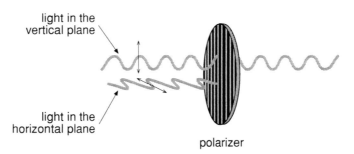

Figure 4: The effect of a polarizer on light

Once the plane of light has passed through the first polarizer, it can continue through a second polarizer (a second piece of polarizing film) only if the orientations of both polarizers are parallel. (See Figure 5.) The orientation of a polarizer is defined as the direction in which most of the polymer molecules are stretched. (The lines of the polarizer shown in Figures 4 and 5 represent the long polymer molecules which make up the polarizer.)

If the orientation of the second polarizer is perpendicular or crossed (at a 90° angle) relative to that of the first polarizer, then the plane of light will be blocked. (See Figure 5.) As the orientation of the second polarizer is rotated from parallel to crossed, less and less light is able to pass through the second polarizer. This concept is illustrated in Part 1 when the polarizing-film circle is placed on the overhead projector. Some of the sections appear light; some appear dark; and still others are at varying levels of light and dark. The amount of light passing through each section of the polarizing-film circle is dependent on its orientation relative to that of the polarizing film sheet attached to the head of the overhead projector. As the polarizing-film circle is rotated 360 degrees, the sections change their orientation relative to the polarizing film attached to the head of the projector and subsequently change from light to dark and back to light.

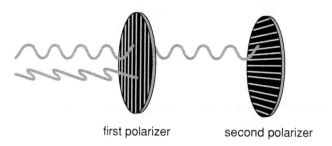

first polarizer   second polarizer

Figure 5: The effect of the second polarizer's orientation on plane polarized light

When a piece of cellophane tape or a cellophane candy wrapper is placed between two crossed polarizers, something surprising occurs. Although the light was blocked previously, now light passes through the second polarizer in the area where the cellophane tape or candy wrapper is located. This light appears on the screen because cellophane has the ability to rotate the plane of light that passes through it. This ability to rotate light is called "optical activity." Therefore, if an optically active material is placed between two crossed polarizers, some light will pass through the second polarizer. This effect is shown in Figure 6.

This wavelength of light is rotated
enough to pass through the
second polarizer.

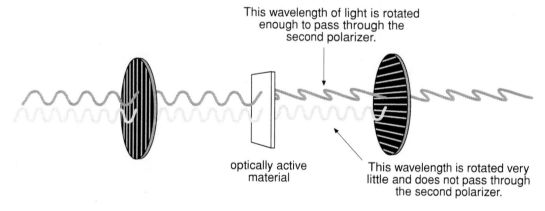

optically active
material

This wavelength is rotated very
little and does not pass through
the second polarizer.

Figure 6: The effect of optically active materials on plane polarized light

Many polymer films are optically active. They have this ability because they are stretched during manufacturing and their molecules become aligned in the direction of the stretch. When light shines through these stretched polymers, the polymer molecules rotate the light waves. This concept is demonstrated in Part 2 when the piece of cellulose acetate is placed between the two crossed polarizers on the overhead projector and no light appears on the screen. After heating and stretching the piece of cellulose acetate, light appears on the screen where the polymer has been stretched. Transparent, molded plastic objects (plastic petri dishes, plastic protractors, clear L'eggs pantyhose eggs, polystyrene drinking cups, etc.) are also optically active and give results that are similar to the stretched cellulose acetate.

In Part 3, the optical activity of the cellophane tape is utilized in making a kaleidoscope. As additional layers of cellophane are placed between the crossed polarizers, the degree of rotation of the wavelengths of light is increased as more and more molecules of cellophane interact with light of various wavelengths.

Another characteristic of optically active substances is that they do not rotate all wavelengths of light the same amount. Because of this difference in the degree of rotation, certain frequencies (colors) of light will not be allowed to pass through the second polarizer due to their orientation. Those wavelengths that do pass through the second polarizer will appear as a particular color. This happens in the activity when the outer polarizing-film circle of the kaleidoscope is rotated; as the orientation of the polarizer changes, different wavelengths are allowed to pass through and different colors appear. With every 90° rotation, the visible light switches from one color to its complementary color.

Key Science Concepts

- optical activity
- plane polarized light
- polymers and their properties

Cross-Curricular Integration

Language Arts
Have students write stories or poems about color or the colored patterns they saw in the kaleidoscope.

Have students create a commercial/advertisement to use during the sale of the kaleidoscopes to the school. (See Mathematics.)

Mathematics
Have students make and sell the kaleidoscopes to students in school. Calculate the amount of profit or loss from the sale.

References

Becker, R., Kirkwood High School, Kirkwood, MO, "Kaleidoscoptical Activity," personal communication.

Ihde, J., West High School, Wausau, WI, personal communication.

Rodriguez, F.; Mathias, L.J.; Kroschwitz, J.; Carraher, C.E., Jr. "Classroom Demonstrations of Polymer Principles. Part III. Physical States and Transitions," *Journal of Chemical Education.* 1988, 65(4), 352–355.

Sherman, M. "Cellophane Tape Kaleidoscope," Fun With Polymers Handout, 1991.

Woodward, L. *Polymers All Around You;* Terrific Science: Middletown, OH, 1992.

Friendly Plastic

Use a polymer called Friendly Plastic® to create wonderful designs. Simply heat Friendly Plastic and let your imagination run wild. If you don't like your first design, reheat the plastic and reshape.

> **Recommended Grade Level** 4–8
> **Group Size** .... individual
> **Time for Preparation** .... 10 minutes
> **Time for Procedure** .... 20–40 minutes

Materials

Opening Strategy
- different kinds of thermoplastic polymers (e.g., shrink wrap, polyethylene bottles/cups)
- different kinds of thermoset polymers (e.g., handles of pans, Formica™ table top, heat-resistant Tupperware®)

Procedure
Per Class
- Friendly Plastic sticks
- near-boiling water in an electric skillet, hot pot, or coffee maker
- nonmetal heat-resistant container
- non-stick work surface (e.g., waxed paper)
- container of cold water
- cooking oil
- wooden craft sticks
- scissors
- cooking thermometer
- (optional) spatula

Extension
All the materials for the Procedure, plus the following:
- access to an oven instead of the heat sources listed for the Procedure
- oven mitts
- aluminum foil
- cookie sheet
- spatula or egg turner
- Amaco® Jewelry Accessories
- Amaco Spray 'n' Seal® protective sealant
- Super Glue
- 1 or more types of decorations:
  - beads
  - sequins
  - rhinestones
  - feathers

- ° acrylic paints and brushes
- ° permanent markers

Resources

Friendly Plastic can purchased at an art supply store or it can be ordered from Amaco, 4717 West 16th St., Indianapolis, IN 46222, 317/244-6871. Amaco jewelry accessories and protective sealant can also be ordered from Amaco.

Safety and Disposal

Warm Friendly Plastic will stick to fingernail polish, acrylic fingernails, aluminum or other metals, Styrofoam™, polyvinyl chloride, and certain other plastics. Do NOT let the students put the Friendly Plastic into their mouths. It bonds to metal braces. Also, do NOT let them make bracelets or rings because these will harden and be difficult to remove from hands or fingers. Since heat is used to soften the Friendly Plastic polymer, students must be warned about touching the hot plastic and the hot water used to heat it.

Remember when storing Friendly Plastic or figures made from it, the Friendly Plastic will soften or melt when exposed to light or heat such as temperatures reached on a hot summer day in a closed car.

Getting Ready

Heat water in an electric skillet, hot pot, or coffee maker until the temperature reaches 60–66°C (140–150°F). Monitor the temperature with a cooking thermometer. Add one or two drops of cooking oil to the water to prevent the Friendly Plastic from sticking. Pour the hot water into a heat-resistant, nonmetal container. (Friendly Plastic sticks to metal.) During the activity, replenish the water as it cools.

Opening Strategy

Show the students different kinds of polymers and discuss the applications of thermoplastic polymers versus thermoset polymers. Examples of thermoplastic polymers include shrink wrap and polyethylene bottles/cups. Examples of thermoset polymers include handles of pans, Formica table top, and heat-resistant Tupperware.

Procedure

1. Plan the design for your artwork and cut the Friendly Plastic into shapes according to the design. You may want to have several pieces ready to soften.

2. Soften one piece of Friendly Plastic at a time as follows:

   a. Slowly lower the Friendly Plastic into the hot water. If using metallic Friendly Plastic, place the metallic side down.

   b. Leave the Friendly Plastic in the hot water for 30–60 seconds. If using metallic sticks, heat until shiny and almost translucent. Metallic sticks will lose their metallic appearance if softened too long.

   c.   Remove the Friendly Plastic using craft sticks.

3.   Wet your hands with cool water and shape the Friendly Plastic into your design once the plastic pieces have softened.

Keep the plastic moving to prevent it from hardening in your hand. Softened plastic pieces cannot be separated if they are allowed to touch. Handle softened plastic pieces carefully.

4.   Multiple-layer designs may be achieved by stacking the pieces on a spatula and slowly lowering them into the hot water. Do not immerse the pieces totally or some of them may float off of the spatula. Add pieces as needed to complete the design.

5.   To create a new color with nonmetallic plastic sticks, soften the plastic pieces and knead them together. The plastic may have to be resoftened and rekneaded a few times before the color becomes uniform.

6.   To bond two pieces of plastic together, soften both pieces in hot water until they are tacky, then press them firmly together. Place the combined piece in cold water to set.

7.   When the desired shape is formed, place it in cold water for 3–5 minutes to set. If the piece has hardened before the desired shape is formed, place each piece back in the hot water for a few seconds and reshape the plastic pieces. This process of dipping in hot and cold water may be repeated as many times as necessary until the final product is completed.

Extension

1.   Preheat an oven to 94°C (200°F).

2.   Lightly oil a piece of aluminum foil larger than the plastic design and place the foil on a cookie sheet oil-side-up.

3.   Before softening, cut plastic pieces into shapes according to your design.

4.   Place the plastic shapes on the aluminum foil in the desired pattern. Intricate designs may require placement and melting of a few pieces at a time.

5.   Bake the design for 2–4 minutes. The pieces of Friendly Plastic will melt together. The longer the Friendly Plastic is left in the oven, the more inlaid (flat) the surface will become.

Do not leave the plastic pieces in the oven too long or the plastic will begin to bubble and the metallic pieces will lose their metallic appearance.

Remember, in the next step the pieces of Friendly Plastic will be warm.

6.   Using oven mitts, remove the design from the oven. Softened plastic pieces may be carefully molded or texturized by pressing them into an Amaco Jewelry Setting. While the plastic is still warm, embed beads, stones, etc. for positioning only, let them cool, and remove them.

7.   Place the finished piece in cold water for about 3–5 minutes to set.

8.   Once the finished design has set, decorate it using acrylic paints or permanent markers. To protect the painted surfaces, use Amaco Spray 'n' Seal protective sealant.

9.   Decorate the design with beads, sequins, glitter, feathers, etc., or attach it to an Amaco Jewelry Accessory such as a pin back or earring back by gluing it into place using Super Glue. Allow the glue to dry for at least 2 hours before wearing.

Discussion

- Describe the characteristics of Friendly Plastic.
  The plastic is hard and stiff at first. After heating, the plastic becomes very pliable and moldable. Once the plastic cools, it becomes hard and stiff again. The plastic can be heated and cooled multiple times without damaging the plastic.

- Classify Friendly Plastic as a thermoplastic polymer or as a thermoset polymer based on the plastic's characteristics.
  Friendly Plastic is a thermoplastic polymer because it can be molded and remolded without damaging the polymer.

Explanation

Thermoplastic polymers can be molded after being heated. The shape is then fixed upon cooling. The advantage of a thermoplastic is that it can be warmed again, molded into a new shape, and cooled down to fix the shape. This characteristic is due to the fact that these polymers have long, unconnected chains, usually randomly coiled with few or no crosslinks. Because of the polymer molecule's construction, the process of heating, remolding, and cooling can be repeated indefinitely as long as the polymer molecules are not degraded. Low-density polyethylene (used in bowls and cups) behaves in this manner, becoming pliable when warmed but hardening when cooled again. Friendly Plastic is a polyester which is extruded into long strips and cut into smaller pieces.

Key Science Concepts

- polymers and their properties
- thermoplastics/thermoset polymers

Cross-Curricular Integration

Art
Have students design jewelry or other art projects from Friendly Plastic.

Language Arts
Have students design a commercial/advertisement to sell key chains or other Friendly Plastic items to other students.

Mathematics
Design and make key chains or other items to be sold to students. Students should calculate the profit or loss associated with the sale.

References

Sherman, M.C. "Polymers Link Science and Fun," presented at a workshop sponsored in part by the Industrial Sponsors, American Chemical Society, Polymer Chemistry Division, August 1993.

"Thermoplastic and Thermoset Polymers;" *Fun With Chemistry: A Guidebook of K–12 Activities;* Sarquis, M., Sarquis, J., Eds.; Institute for Chemical Education: Madison, WI, 1993; Volume 2, pp 113–119.

Epoxy Putty

How can you bring art into the science classroom? By using a polymer resin called epoxy putty, students can make interesting figures and learn more about this special polymer.

> **Recommended Grade Level** 3–8
> **Group Size** .... individual
> **Time for Preparation** .... 5 minutes
> **Time for Procedure** .... 15 minutes

Materials

Opening Strategy
- handles from pots and pans
- polyethylene bottles, caps, or other products

Procedure
Per Class
- different colors of epoxy putty
- rubbing alcohol (70% isopropyl alcohol solution)
- cotton balls or disposable makeup wipes
- (optional) acrylic or tempera paints
- (optional) paintbrushes
- knife or scissors
- plastic wrap or large zipper-type plastic bags
- Bunsen burner
- tongs
- goggles

Resources

The epoxy putty can be purchased from a hardware or discount department store as SOS Epoxy Putty. Other brands are also available.

Safety and Disposal

Goggles should be worn when performing this activity. Warn students not to get the epoxy putty in their eyes or mouths, since the components of the putty can be harmful. Provide rubbing alcohol for students to use for cleaning their hands after making the epoxy putty figures. Isopropyl alcohol is intended for external use only.

Note all safety warnings on the epoxy putty package and do not let students make bracelets or rings because they will be difficult to remove after hardening. Have students keep the putty on a piece of plastic like a zipper-type plastic bag or plastic wrap because sometimes the putty can be difficult to remove from surfaces.

Getting Ready

Cut the epoxy putty components into pieces about the size of a large walnut. Do not mix the pieces together or the chemical reaction will begin and harden the putty before the students have a chance to mold them.

Opening Strategy

Show students different kinds of polymers. Explain that a thermoset polymer will not melt upon heating once it has been formed. Its structure has crosslinking from one chain to the next. A thermoplastic polymer will melt upon heating, because its structure consists of independent, long molecules. Discuss the application of thermoset polymers versus thermoplastic polymers. Examples of thermoset polymers include handles of pans, Formica tabletops, etc. Possible examples of thermoplastic polymers include Friendly Plastic®, polyethylene bottles/cups, etc.

Procedure

1. Place a piece of plastic wrap or a large, zipper-type plastic bag on the bench or desktop to prevent the epoxy putty from sticking.

2. Knead, roll, twist, and fold the two component pieces of epoxy putty in your hands until the putty takes on a uniform color and begins to feel warm. Do not mix for more than 2 minutes or the putty may become too hard to mold.

3. Reserve a small amount of the putty to use in Step 6.

4. Quickly mold the mixed putty into different shapes. Within 5 minutes the putty will set and become very hard. Once this has happened, the putty cannot be remolded.

5. (optional) Once hardened, use acrylic or tempera paints to paint the figure.

 Allow the epoxy putty to set for at least one day before performing the following combustion test. Perform this test in an exhaust hood using very small samples to minimize possible contact with potentially toxic fumes. Precautions should also be taken to avoid contact with molten plastic, which can cause a skin burn.

6. Once the epoxy putty has hardened, show that it is not affected by heat by using tongs to hold a small amount of putty (saved in Step 3) in the flame of a Bunsen burner. Observe what happens to the putty.

Extensions

- Show the difference between exothermic and endothermic reactions by comparing the epoxy putty to Friendly Plastic, a thermoplastic polymer. (See Activity 19.) As the epoxy putty sets, it radiates heat and therefore is an example of an exothermic reaction, unlike the Friendly Plastic, which needs to be heated before it can be molded. Friendly Plastic is an example of an endothermic physical change.

- The formation of epoxy putty can be illustrated with a kinesthetic demonstration using six students. Have three of the students stand with their hands on their hips. These students represent the diepoxy molecules, and each loop of their arms represents one epoxy group. The other three students represent the diamine molecules. Have them stand with both hands out. Each hand represents an amine group. To cause the reaction, one of the diamine molecules must open the epoxy ring (pull the student's arm so that it is now out) and then join hands. (See Figure 1.) When the students try to open the ring, the student representing the diepoxy molecule should try to resist, but eventually allow the ring to open. This demonstrates that heat is released when the ring is opened. This reaction continues until all of the monomer molecules have reacted.

Figure 1: Kinesthetic demonstration of diepoxy molecules, diamine molecules, and epoxy putty molecule

Discussion

- Ask students to describe the temperature of the reaction as the two pieces of epoxy putty are kneaded together. Ask them to classify the reaction as exothermic or endothermic.
  As the putty is kneaded together, it becomes warm. This is an exothermic reaction.

- Based on the flame test in Step 6, ask the students to classify the epoxy putty as a thermoplastic or as a thermoset polymer.
  Since the putty can not be reheated and remolded after it has set, it is a thermoset polymer.

- Discuss some uses of epoxy putty.
  Epoxy resins are used for electrical insulators, dies for stamping metal sheets, electronic assemblies, and adhesives.

Explanation

Epoxy putty is a polymer that is made when a molecule containing two epoxy groups (diepoxy, see Figure 2) and a molecule containing two amine groups (diamine) react. In addition to the formation of a linear chain, sometimes the diamine molecule will react with epoxy groups on different chains, causing them to bond together in a complex three-dimensional network. This three-dimensional network is what makes the epoxy putty become hard and rigid. Epoxy resins are characterized by excellent chemical resistance, adhesion to glass and metals, electrical insulation properties, and ease and precision of fabrication.

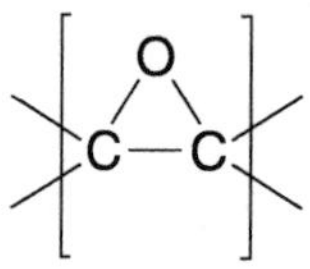

Figure 2: An epoxy group

Because of their good adhesive properties, epoxies are commonly used in protective coatings. Due to their high resistance to heat and chemicals, epoxy resins are very useful for metal-to-metal bonding. Because of the small density change on curing and because of their excellent electrical properties, epoxy resins are used as potting or encapsulating compositions for the protection of delicate electronic assemblies from the thermal and mechanical shock of rocket flight. Due to their dimensional stability and toughness, epoxies are used extensively as dies for stamping metal forms, such as automobile gas tanks from metal sheeting. By combining epoxies, especially the higher-performance types, with fibers of glass or carbon, strong composites can be made. These composites are of increasing importance in aerospace applications and sports equipment.

Key Science Concepts

- epoxies
- exothermic/endothermic reactions
- polymers and their properties

Cross-Curricular Integration

Art
Have the students use the putty to create an art project.

Home, Safety, and Career
Have students brainstorm possible uses of epoxy resins.

References

Parker, S.P. *McGraw-Hill Encyclopedia of Chemistry;* McGraw-Hill: New York, NY, 1983; pp 796–797.

Sherman, M.C. "Polymers Link Science and Fun," presentation at workshop sponsored in part by the Industrial Sponsors, American Chemical Society, Polymer Chemistry Division, August 1993.

The Amazing Shrinking Plastic | 21

How do companies fit plastic so tightly around packages? They use a plastic called "shrink wrap" that shrinks when it is heated. In this activity, students determine the amount of shrinkage in a polystyrene sheet.

> **Recommended Grade Level** 4–12
> **Group Size** .... individual
> **Time for Preparation** .... 10 minutes
> **Time for Procedure** .... 30–40 minutes

Materials

Opening Strategy
- example of a shrink-wrapped item
- examples of plastics before and after shrinking

Procedure
Per Class
- scissors
- cardboard
- rulers
- fine-tipped permanent markers
- 1 or more of the following types of shrinkable plastics:
  - plastic salad or bakery boxes (with a #6 recycle code)
  - clear, plastic lid from a yogurt container (with a #6 recycle code)
  - Shrinky Dinks®
- aluminum foil or cookie sheet
- access to an oven
- oven mitt or tongs
- balance

Variations
- hole punch

Resources

Shrinky Dinks, manufactured by Colorforms, Ramsey, NJ 07446, and Milton Bradley, Springfield, MA 01101, can be purchased from a toy or department store.

Getting Ready

Cut pieces of cardboard into rectangles for the students to use as patterns for cutting the plastic (5-cm x 10-cm or other size to fit the type of plastic source you are using). If using salad or bakery boxes as the source of plastic (as shown in Figure 1), use the flat surface of the plastic containers.

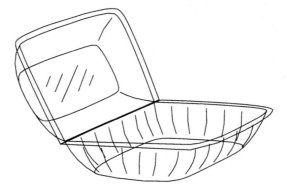

Figure 1: Polystyrene container for salad or bakery items

Opening Strategy

Explain to students that several types of plastics shrink when heated in an oven. Show a common example of a "shrink-wrapped" item. Also show samples of plastic before and after shrinking. Ask the students to suggest ways in which they could determine the amount (percent or fraction) of shrinkage a plastic undergoes when heated. Discuss methods and elicit suggestions for a procedure.

Procedure

Part 1: How Much Shrinkage?

1. Use the cardboard patterns prepared in Getting Ready to cut out a piece of shrinkable plastic.

2. Using a fine-tipped, permanent marker, mark an L for length, a W for width, and your name on the plastic cutout. Measure and record the dimensions of the sample.

3. (optional) Trace the outline of the plastic piece on a sheet of paper and denote the length and width of the plastic.

4. Determine and record the mass of the plastic piece.

5. Collect the plastic samples and place them on aluminum foil or a cookie sheet. Heat them for about 5 minutes in a 170°C (350°F) oven. Use an oven mitt or tongs to remove the plastic pieces from the oven and allow them to cool thoroughly before handling.

6. Measure the length and width of the shrunken plastic.

7. (optional) Compare dimensions to outline traced in Step 3, if done.

8. Determine the change in the dimensions of the plastic sample by subtracting. Then calculate the percent (or the fractional) change for each dimension using the following formula:

$$\% \text{ change in length (or width)} = \frac{\text{difference in length (or width)}}{\text{length (or width) before heating}} \times 100$$

9. (optional) Determine the area (L x W) of the plastic piece before heating and after heating and calculate the percent change in area.

10. Determine the mass of the shrunken plastic and calculate the percent change in mass using the following formula:

$$\% \text{ change in mass} = \frac{\text{difference in mass}}{\text{mass before heating}} \times 100$$

Variations

- Compare the percent of shrinkage in 5 minutes of heating at different oven temperatures (250°F, 300°F, 350°F, and 400°F).

- Make earrings or pendants by cutting interesting shapes, coloring them with permanent markers, and shrinking them. Before heating, use a hole punch to make holes for hanging.

Discussion

- Discuss how the length and width of the sample could change while the mass of the plastic sample remains constant.
  Since the shrinkage of the plastic sample is a physical change, the mass should not change. The mass would only change if a new compound was formed. The shrinking is just the polymer strands returning to a more random orientation.

- Ask the students how the thickness of the plastic sample changed due to the heating process.
  The plastic sample became much thicker after shrinking.

Sample Data

	Polystyrene			
Sample	Before Shrinking	After Shrinking	Difference	Percent Change
length (L)	4.5 cm	1.8 cm	2.7 cm	60%
width (W)	4.5 cm	1.2 cm	3.3 cm	73%
mass	0.53 g	0.53 g	0.0 g	0%

Explanation

Depending upon how they are manufactured, polystyrene and certain other polymers can have the ability to shrink when heated. The shrinking ability of polystyrene and other shrinkable plastics is somewhat unusual. Most solids, when heated, either expand before they melt into liquids (for example, metals) or decompose (for example, wood into charcoal). However, when the shrinkable polystyrene is heated at low temperatures, it does not decompose to form new products; the molecules merely return to their original (not stretched) configurations. This means that no change in mass is expected.

Polystyrene exhibits its shrinking nature due to the way it is manufactured. As it is produced, the polystyrene is heated, stretched out into a film, then quickly cooled. The sudden cooling "freezes" the long polymer molecules in a stretched-out configuration. To visualize this process, imagine how a person might appear if suddenly asked to freeze while in the middle of doing jumping jacks. When these plastics are heated once again, the molecules within them are released from their "frozen" configurations; they return to their original dimensions, resulting in the observed shrinkage.

The type of polystyrene used in this activity is made by first heating the solid polymer (which consists of many long coiled strands) until it melts. The melt is forced to flow (extruded) uniformly up through a round metal slit (a die), and so is shaped as a thin tube. (See Figure 2.) At the start-up, the top of the tube is pulled together to form a bubble. Compressed air from a line within the die forces the bubble away from the die (Thus this is a blown film) at a speed greater than that of the polymer flow into the die. This stretches the film in the direction of the machine (axially oriented). Blowing up the bubble to 1.5 to three times the diameter of the die stretches it in a direction perpendicular to the axial direction (radially oriented). By the time the tubular bubble reaches the top of the assembly, it has cooled enough to "lock" the strands into their stretched dimension, and it is collapsed to a flat, two-layer sheet.

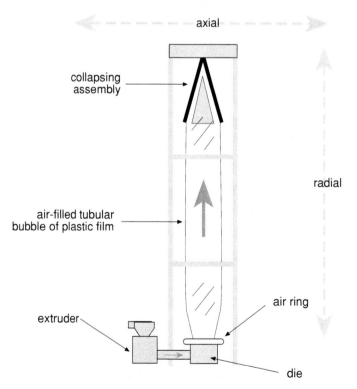

Figure 2: Plastic films are made by extruding the melted polymer, stretching the tubular bubble, and collapsing the cooling bubble into a flat, two-layer sheet.

The result is a film stretched in two directions (biaxially oriented). With the polymer strands so aligned, the film has increased tensile strength, lower permeability due to tighter alignment of the strands, and improved impact resistance, clarity, and lightness of the container. (Its clarity and strength properties make it ideal for blister packs, candy and pastry trays, and related food packages.) Upon reheating to 163°C (325°F), the film resoftens and the strands are free to return to their unstretched state.

Key Science Concepts

- effects of heat
- polymers and their properties

Cross-Curricular Integration

Art
Using permanent markers, draw and color pictures on the polystyrene before it is heated.

Home, Safety, and Career
Discuss with the students the advantages and disadvantages of using plastic for packaging food.

Language Arts
Write short stories describing the adventures of someone who has been shrunk to a third of his/her original size.

References

Ihde, J., West High School, Wausau, WI, personal communication.

Rodriguez, F. "Classroom Demonstrations of Polymer Principles," *Journal of Chemical Education.* 1990, 69(9), 784–788.

Sherman, M.C. "Polymers Link Science and Fun," presentation at a workshop sponsored in part by the Industrial Sponsors, American Chemical Society, Polymer Chemistry Division, August 1993.

"Shrinkable Plastics," *Fun With Chemistry: A Guidebook of K–12 Activities;* Sarquis, M., Sarquis, J., Eds.; Institute for Chemical Education: Madison, WI, 1993; Vol. 2, pp 101–105.

Taking the Foam Out of Styrofoam

22

What can you do with Styrofoam™ or Eco-foam® packing peanuts besides packing? Here is an activity that will make them "disappear."

> Recommended Grade Level 6–12
> Group Size .... 1–4 students
> Time for Preparation .... none
> Time for Procedure .... 10–15 minutes

Materials

Opening Strategy
- Styrofoam cup
- polystyrene cup

Procedure, Part 1
Per Group
- enough Styrofoam packing peanuts to fill a 600-mL beaker
- 600-mL beaker
- about 10 mL acetone
- 250-mL beaker
- glass stirring rod
- (optional) a shopping bag full of Styrofoam packing peanuts
- goggles

Procedure, Part 2
Per Group
- enough corn starch packing peanuts (Eco-foam) to fill a 600-mL beaker
- 600-mL beaker
- 250-mL beaker
- stirring rod or stick

Resources

Acetone can be purchased from a hardware store or chemical supply company such as Flinn Scientific, P.O. Box 219, Batavia, IL 60510-0219, 800/452-1261.

- acetone—catalog # A0009 for 500 mL

You may receive Eco-foam in packaging from an environmentally conscious company. It can be purchased from Frey Scientific, 905 Hickory Lane, P.O. Box 8101, Mansfield, OH 44901, 800/225-FREY.

- Eco-foam—catalog # 20641 for 12.5 lbs of packing peanuts

Safety and Disposal

Goggles should be worn for Part 1. Acetone is very flammable. Keep the acetone away from flames and heat, which could cause it to ignite. Acetone vapors are irritating to the eyes and respiratory system, and the liquid is toxic if ingested. Use acetone only in a well-ventilated area. Dispose of acetone by placing the container in a working fume hood to evaporate, or by pouring it down the drain with large amounts of water.

Opening Strategy

Show the class a clear, polystyrene cup and a Styrofoam hot-beverage cup. Explain to them that these two cups are made from the same polymer, polystyrene, but they don't look the same. Ask students to explain how these cups are different. Once they have guessed that the hot-beverage cup has a gas trapped in it, ask them to suggest ways of releasing the air that is trapped.

Procedure

Part 1: Styrofoam and Acetone

1. Pour acetone into a 250-mL beaker to a height of about 2 mm.

2. Show students a 600-mL beaker full of Styrofoam packing peanuts and ask how many peanuts they think will fit into the 250-mL beaker containing the thin layer of acetone.

3. Add the Styrofoam peanuts to the 250-mL beaker a few at a time, allowing each batch to collapse before adding more. Have students keep a count of how many peanuts are added. Make sure that all of the peanuts touch the acetone as they are added. Keep adding peanuts until all of them have collapsed.

4. (optional) For a more dramatic demonstration, keep a shopping bag full of Styrofoam peanuts out of sight until all of the peanuts from the 600-mL beaker have collapsed in the acetone. Then bring out the bag and keep adding peanuts until no more will fit into the beaker.

Part 2: Eco-Foam and Water

1. Pour water into a 250-mL beaker to a height of about 2 mm.

2. Show students a 600-mL beaker full of Eco-foam packing peanuts and ask how many peanuts they think will fit into the 250-mL beaker containing the thin layer of water.

3. Add the Eco-foam peanuts to the 250-mL beaker a few at a time, allowing each batch to collapse before adding more. Have students keep a count of how many peanuts are added. Make sure that all of the peanuts touch the water as they are added. Keep adding peanuts until no more will collapse.

Discussion

- Explain the reason for the change in volume of the peanuts after they are mixed with the solvents.
  The foam packing peanuts consist of a gas trapped inside a structure made of a polymer such as polystyrene or corn starch. When the foam peanuts are placed in the appropriate solvent (acetone for polystyrene and water for corn starch), the trapped gas escapes.

- Discuss the significance of reducing the volume of packing material as shown in this activity. *By reducing the volume of the packing material, the volume that the material will occupy in a landfill is also reduced.*

Explanation

When Styrofoam is placed in a beaker containing acetone, the acetone molecules interact with the foam. The acetone weakens the attractions that give the Styrofoam its rigid shape and the result is a flexible soft glob. The volume of the Styrofoam decreases because the rigid structure collapses. The sticky polystyrene residue may be recovered, washed, and observed. The residue no longer has the gas incorporated within it and will eventually become hard. A relatively small amount of acetone will alter large amounts of Styrofoam.

When the Eco-foam is placed in a beaker containing water, the corn starch component of the foam begins to dissolve in the water. The volume of the foam decreases because the trapped gas escapes and the starch dissolves.

Key Science Concepts

- chemical and physical changes
- polymers and their properties

Cross-Curricular Integration

Art
Have students create sculptures or projects using Styrofoam.

Home, Safety, and Career
Have students write to local fast food restaurants that use Styrofoam to find out if they are conducting any recycling of polystyrene.

Language Arts
Have students write reports on the "life cycle" of a Styrofoam cup from production to disposal.

References

Sherman, M.C. "Polymers Link Science and Fun," presentation at a workshop sponsored in part by the Industrial Sponsors, American Chemical Society, Polymer Chemistry Division, August 1993.

Molding Plastics

Have you ever wondered how a 2-L bottle gets its shape? Students explore one type of plastic molding, extrusion blow molding, and make their own plastic bottles.

Recommended Grade Level 7–12
Group Size .... 1–4 students
Time for Preparation .... none
Time for Procedure .... 35–45 minutes

Materials

Opening Strategy
Per Class
- 1-L bottle
- balloon
- push pin or hot nail

Procedure
Per Group
- 50-mL beaker or wide-mouthed bottle

 The Quorpak bottle listed in Resources will work well.

- vegetable oil
- 6-in to 10-in length of extruded polyethylene tubing with ¼-in outer diameter
- heat gun
- pliers or crucible tongs
- scissors
- (optional) pipette
- goggles

Resources

Polyethylene tubing and 1-oz glass bottles can be purchased from a chemical supply company such as Fisher Scientific, 9403 Kenwood Road C-208, Cincinnati, OH 45242, 800/766-7000.

- Nalgene 489 polyethylene tubing, ¼-in o.d.— catalog # 14-176-121 for 100 feet
- Quorpak™ clear, wide-mouthed French square bottles—catalog # 03-327-14B for 48 bottles

Polyethylene tubing can also be purchased at hardware or beverage supply stores.

Safety and Disposal

Goggles should be worn when performing this activity. Exercise caution when using a heat gun to heat the tubing.

Opening Strategy

Demonstrate the concept of blow molding with a 1-L bottle and a balloon. Use a push pin or hot nail to punch a small hole (about 1 cm in diameter) near the bottom of the bottle. Push the uninflated balloon into the bottle and stretch the open end of the balloon back over the bottle's mouth. Inflate the balloon and hold your hand over the balloon opening to keep the balloon inflated inside the bottle. Tell the students that the balloon represents a plastic form that has been heated to the temperature at which it becomes flexible (what polymer chemists call the glass transition temperature) and inflated to take on the shape of the mold.

Procedure

1. Lightly coat the inside of the 1-oz bottle or beaker with vegetable oil.

2. Gently heat the bottom ¼ inch of the tubing with a heat gun.

3. Remove the tube from the heat source.

4. Using a pair of pliers or tongs, crimp and seal the heated end of the tubing.

5. Continue heating just above the sealed end of the tubing for a length equal to the height of the bottle being used until the plastic becomes clear and colorless (molten.)
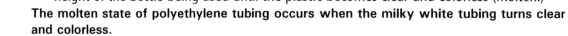
The molten state of polyethylene tubing occurs when the milky white tubing turns clear and colorless.

6. Lower the molten tubing into the bottle so that the heated section is below the mouth of the bottle.

7. Blow gently into the cold end of the tube so that the molten end (the end in the bottle) expands.
It may take several tries before you can inflate a bottle without blowing out one side. The best results come from heating the plastic uniformly and blowing gently.

8. Once the tubing has filled the bottle, put a finger over the cold end of the tube to keep the tubing expanded in the mold for about 20–30 seconds.

9. Carefully pull the expanded tubing back through the mouth of the bottle. The plastic should be flexible enough to allow this.

10. Cut off the excess tubing.

11. Test your molded "bottle" for its ability to hold water. If the opening of the bottle is small, you may need to use a pipette to fill it.

Discussion

• Discuss reasons for leaking if a blow-molded bottle will not hold water. Have students think of ways to improve the technique to avoid this problem.

• Pass around commercially blown bottles and have students theorize what their molds must have looked like.

Explanation

Of the billions of plastic bottles used annually in the U.S., almost all are made by some method of blow molding. The most common blow molding process is extrusion blow molding. This process uses molten plastic that is formed into a tube (commonly called a parison) and inflated against a cold mold. When the molten plastic touches the sides of the cold mold, it cools and assumes the inside dimensions of the mold. The blow molding process simulated in this activity is the extrusion blow molding process. The polyethylene tubing represents a parison and the 1-oz bottle or beaker was used as the mold.

Partially crystalline materials like HDPE and polypropylene (PP) have a high melt strength (They are taffy-like when molten) and crystallize very quickly, making them usable in the extrusion blow molding process. Common examples of products blow molded from HDPE include detergent bottles, shampoo bottles, and milk bottles.

A second type of blow molding, injection stretch blow molding, uses a small, injection molded preform of the final bottle. The preform is heated to its glass transition temperature and then, while being inflated in a cold mold, is mechanically stretched along its vertical axis. This process gives the bottle toughness and makes it less permeable to moisture.

Although many types of plastic can be blow molded, the two that are predominately used to make bottles are polyethylene terephthalate (PET) and high-density polyethylene (HDPE). PET, the polymer used in 2-L soft-drink bottles, is made by combining ethylene glycol with terephthalic acid to form a polyester. PET is an amorphous polymer like polyvinyl chloride (PVC) and polystyrene (PS). These polymers have very little melt strength (They flow like water when molten), making them impossible to use in extrusion blow molding. The injection stretch blow molding process is instead used for PET, PVC, and PS.

Key Science Concept

- methods of polymer molding

Cross-Curricular Integration

Language Arts
- Have students write research reports about the various methods used to manufacture the plastic products we use.

References

Polymer Chemistry: A Teaching Package for Pre-College Teachers; National Science Teachers Association: Washington, D.C., 1989.

Rodriguez, F. "Classroom Demonstration of Polymer Principles," *Journal of Chemical Education.* 1992, 69(11), 915–920.